KEY: ☒ COMPLETED
       ⊟ UNCOMPLETED

DAILY CALLS

① X —	② X —	③ X —
④ X —	⑤ X —	⑥ X —
⑦ X —	⑧ X —	⑨ X —
⑩ X —	⑪ X —	⑫ X —
⑬ X —	⑭ X —	⑮ X —

"OOPS I FORGOT" - CARRY OVER TOMORROW

TO DO LIST #'S -

DAILY CALL #'S -

DAILY TASKS

DATE:

I0404800

① X —
② X —
③ X —
④ X —
⑤ X —
⑥ X —
⑦ X —
⑧ X —
⑨ X —
⑩ X —
⑪ X —
⑫ X —
⑬ X —
⑭ X —
⑮ X —
⑯ X —
⑰ X —
⑱ X —
⑲ X —
⑳ X —
㉑ X —
㉒ X —
㉓ X —
㉔ X —
㉕ X —

KEY: ☒ COMPLETED
⊟ UNCOMPLETED

DAILY CALLS

① X —	② X —	③ X —
④ X —	⑤ X —	⑥ X —
⑦ X —	⑧ X —	⑨ X —
⑩ X —	⑪ X —	⑫ X —
⑬ X —	⑭ X —	⑮ X —

"OOPS I FORGOT" - CARRY OVER TOMORROW

TO DO LIST #'S -

DAILY CALL #'S -

DAILY TASKS

DATE:

① X —
② X —
③ X —
④ X —
⑤ X —
⑥ X —
⑦ X —
⑧ X —
⑨ X —
⑩ X —
⑪ X —
⑫ X —
⑬ X —
⑭ X —
⑮ X —
⑯ X —
⑰ X —
⑱ X —
⑲ X —
⑳ X —
㉑ X —
㉒ X —
㉓ X —
㉔ X —
㉕ X —

KEY: [X] COMPLETED
      [—] UNCOMPLETED

DAILY CALLS

(1) [X] [—]   (2) [X] [—]   (3) [X] [—]

(4) [X] [—]   (5) [X] [—]   (6) [X] [—]

(7) [X] [—]   (8) [X] [—]   (9) [X] [—]

(10) [X] [—] (11) [X] [—] (12) [X] [—]

(13) [X] [—] (14) [X] [—] (15) [X] [—]

"OOPS I FORGOT" - CARRY OVER TOMORROW

TO DO LIST #'S -

DAILY CALL #'S -

DAILY TASKS

DATE:

(1) [X] [—]
(2) [X] [—]
(3) [X] [—]
(4) [X] [—]
(5) [X] [—]
(6) [X] [—]
(7) [X] [—]
(8) [X] [—]
(9) [X] [—]
(10) [X] [—]
(11) [X] [—]
(12) [X] [—]
(13) [X] [—]
(14) [X] [—]
(15) [X] [—]
(16) [X] [—]
(17) [X] [—]
(18) [X] [—]
(19) [X] [—]
(20) [X] [—]
(21) [X] [—]
(22) [X] [—]
(23) [X] [—]
(24) [X] [—]
(25) [X] [—]

KEY: [X] COMPLETED
[—] UNCOMPLETED

DAILY CALLS

① [X] [—]	② [X] [—]	③ [X] [—]
④ [X] [—]	⑤ [X] [—]	⑥ [X] [—]
⑦ [X] [—]	⑧ [X] [—]	⑨ [X] [—]
⑩ [X] [—]	⑪ [X] [—]	⑫ [X] [—]
⑬ [X] [—]	⑭ [X] [—]	⑮ [X] [—]

"OOPS I FORGOT" - CARRY OVER TOMORROW

TO DO LIST #'S -

DAILY CALL #'S -

DAILY TASKS

DATE:

① [X] [—]
② [X] [—]
③ [X] [—]
④ [X] [—]
⑤ [X] [—]
⑥ [X] [—]
⑦ [X] [—]
⑧ [X] [—]
⑨ [X] [—]
⑩ [X] [—]
⑪ [X] [—]
⑫ [X] [—]
⑬ [X] [—]
⑭ [X] [—]
⑮ [X] [—]
⑯ [X] [—]
⑰ [X] [—]
⑱ [X] [—]
⑲ [X] [—]
⑳ [X] [—]
㉑ [X] [—]
㉒ [X] [—]
㉓ [X] [—]
㉔ [X] [—]
㉕ [X] [—]

KEY: ☒ COMPLETED
☐— UNCOMPLETED

DAILY CALLS

(1) ☒ ☐—	(2) ☒ ☐—	(3) ☒ ☐—
(4) ☒ ☐—	(5) ☒ ☐—	(6) ☒ ☐—
(7) ☒ ☐—	(8) ☒ ☐—	(9) ☒ ☐—
(10) ☒ ☐—	(11) ☒ ☐—	(12) ☒ ☐—
(13) ☒ ☐—	(14) ☒ ☐—	(15) ☒ ☐—

"OOPS I FORGOT" - CARRY OVER TOMORROW

TO DO LIST #'S -

DAILY CALL #'S -

DAILY TASKS

DATE:

1. ☒ ☐—
2. ☒ ☐—
3. ☒ ☐—
4. ☒ ☐—
5. ☒ ☐—
6. ☒ ☐—
7. ☒ ☐—
8. ☒ ☐—
9. ☒ ☐—
10. ☒ ☐—
11. ☒ ☐—
12. ☒ ☐—
13. ☒ ☐—
14. ☒ ☐—
15. ☒ ☐—
16. ☒ ☐—
17. ☒ ☐—
18. ☒ ☐—
19. ☒ ☐—
20. ☒ ☐—
21. ☒ ☐—
22. ☒ ☐—
23. ☒ ☐—
24. ☒ ☐—
25. ☒ ☐—

KEY: ☒ COMPLETED
⊟ UNCOMPLETED

DAILY CALLS

① X —
② X —
③ X —
④ X —
⑤ X —
⑥ X —
⑦ X —
⑧ X —
⑨ X —
⑩ X —
⑪ X —
⑫ X —
⑬ X —
⑭ X —
⑮ X —

"OOPS I FORGOT" - CARRY OVER TOMORROW

TO DO LIST #'S -

DAILY CALL #'S -

DAILY TASKS

DATE:

① X —
② X —
③ X —
④ X —
⑤ X —
⑥ X —
⑦ X —
⑧ X —
⑨ X —
⑩ X —
⑪ X —
⑫ X —
⑬ X —
⑭ X —
⑮ X —
⑯ X —
⑰ X —
⑱ X —
⑲ X —
⑳ X —
㉑ X —
㉒ X —
㉓ X —
㉔ X —
㉕ X —

KEY: ☒ COMPLETED
⊟ UNCOMPLETED

DAILY CALLS

① X — ② X — ③ X —

④ X — ⑤ X — ⑥ X —

⑦ X — ⑧ X — ⑨ X —

⑩ X — ⑪ X — ⑫ X —

⑬ X — ⑭ X — ⑮ X —

"OOPS I FORGOT" - CARRY OVER TOMORROW

TO DO LIST #'S -

DAILY CALL #'S -

DAILY TASKS

DATE:

① X —
② X —
③ X —
④ X —
⑤ X —
⑥ X —
⑦ X —
⑧ X —
⑨ X —
⑩ X —
⑪ X —
⑫ X —
⑬ X —
⑭ X —
⑮ X —
⑯ X —
⑰ X —
⑱ X —
⑲ X —
⑳ X —
㉑ X —
㉒ X —
㉓ X —
㉔ X —
㉕ X —

KEY: ☒ COMPLETED
☐ UNCOMPLETED

DAILY CALLS

① X —   ② X —   ③ X —

④ X —   ⑤ X —   ⑥ X —

⑦ X —   ⑧ X —   ⑨ X —

⑩ X —   ⑪ X —   ⑫ X —

⑬ X —   ⑭ X —   ⑮ X —

"OOPS I FORGOT" - CARRY OVER TOMORROW

TO DO LIST #'S -

DAILY CALL #'S -

DAILY TASKS

DATE:

1. X —
2. X —
3. X —
4. X —
5. X —
6. X —
7. X —
8. X —
9. X —
10. X —
11. X —
12. X —
13. X —
14. X —
15. X —
16. X —
17. X —
18. X —
19. X —
20. X —
21. X —
22. X —
23. X —
24. X —
25. X —

KEY: [X] COMPLETED
[—] UNCOMPLETED

DAILY CALLS

(1) [X] [—]	(2) [X] [—]	(3) [X] [—]
(4) [X] [—]	(5) [X] [—]	(6) [X] [—]
(7) [X] [—]	(8) [X] [—]	(9) [X] [—]
(10) [X] [—]	(11) [X] [—]	(12) [X] [—]
(13) [X] [—]	(14) [X] [—]	(15) [X] [—]

"OOPS I FORGOT" - CARRY OVER TOMORROW

TO DO LIST #'S -

DAILY CALL #'S -

DAILY TASKS

DATE:

(1) [X] [—]
(2) [X] [—]
(3) [X] [—]
(4) [X] [—]
(5) [X] [—]
(6) [X] [—]
(7) [X] [—]
(8) [X] [—]
(9) [X] [—]
(10) [X] [—]
(11) [X] [—]
(12) [X] [—]
(13) [X] [—]
(14) [X] [—]
(15) [X] [—]
(16) [X] [—]
(17) [X] [—]
(18) [X] [—]
(19) [X] [—]
(20) [X] [—]
(21) [X] [—]
(22) [X] [—]
(23) [X] [—]
(24) [X] [—]
(25) [X] [—]

KEY: ☒ COMPLETED
☐ UNCOMPLETED

DAILY CALLS

① X ☐	② X ☐	③ X ☐
④ X ☐	⑤ X ☐	⑥ X ☐
⑦ X ☐	⑧ X ☐	⑨ X ☐
⑩ X ☐	⑪ X ☐	⑫ X ☐
⑬ X ☐	⑭ X ☐	⑮ X ☐

"OOPS I FORGOT" - CARRY OVER TOMORROW

TO DO LIST #'S -

DAILY CALL #'S -

DAILY TASKS
DATE:

① X ☐
② X ☐
③ X ☐
④ X ☐
⑤ X ☐
⑥ X ☐
⑦ X ☐
⑧ X ☐
⑨ X ☐
⑩ X ☐
⑪ X ☐
⑫ X ☐
⑬ X ☐
⑭ X ☐
⑮ X ☐
⑯ X ☐
⑰ X ☐
⑱ X ☐
⑲ X ☐
⑳ X ☐
㉑ X ☐
㉒ X ☐
㉓ X ☐
㉔ X ☐
㉕ X ☐

KEY: ☒ COMPLETED
⊟ UNCOMPLETED

DAILY CALLS

① X ⊟	② X ⊟	③ X ⊟
④ X ⊟	⑤ X ⊟	⑥ X ⊟
⑦ X ⊟	⑧ X ⊟	⑨ X ⊟
⑩ X ⊟	⑪ X ⊟	⑫ X ⊟
⑬ X ⊟	⑭ X ⊟	⑮ X ⊟

"OOPS I FORGOT" - CARRY OVER TOMORROW

TO DO LIST #'S -

DAILY CALL #'S -

DAILY TASKS

DATE:

① X ⊟
② X ⊟
③ X ⊟
④ X ⊟
⑤ X ⊟
⑥ X ⊟
⑦ X ⊟
⑧ X ⊟
⑨ X ⊟
⑩ X ⊟
⑪ X ⊟
⑫ X ⊟
⑬ X ⊟
⑭ X ⊟
⑮ X ⊟
⑯ X ⊟
⑰ X ⊟
⑱ X ⊟
⑲ X ⊟
⑳ X ⊟
㉑ X ⊟
㉒ X ⊟
㉓ X ⊟
㉔ X ⊟
㉕ X ⊟

KEY: ☒ COMPLETED
☐ UNCOMPLETED

DAILY CALLS

① ☒ ☐   ② ☒ ☐   ③ ☒ ☐

④ ☒ ☐   ⑤ ☒ ☐   ⑥ ☒ ☐

⑦ ☒ ☐   ⑧ ☒ ☐   ⑨ ☒ ☐

⑩ ☒ ☐   ⑪ ☒ ☐   ⑫ ☒ ☐

⑬ ☒ ☐   ⑭ ☒ ☐   ⑮ ☒ ☐

"OOPS I FORGOT" - CARRY OVER TOMORROW

TO DO LIST #'S -

DAILY CALL #'S -

DAILY TASKS

DATE:

① ☒ ☐
② ☒ ☐
③ ☒ ☐
④ ☒ ☐
⑤ ☒ ☐
⑥ ☒ ☐
⑦ ☒ ☐
⑧ ☒ ☐
⑨ ☒ ☐
⑩ ☒ ☐
⑪ ☒ ☐
⑫ ☒ ☐
⑬ ☒ ☐
⑭ ☒ ☐
⑮ ☒ ☐
⑯ ☒ ☐
⑰ ☒ ☐
⑱ ☒ ☐
⑲ ☒ ☐
⑳ ☒ ☐
㉑ ☒ ☐
㉒ ☒ ☐
㉓ ☒ ☐
㉔ ☒ ☐
㉕ ☒ ☐

KEY: [X] COMPLETED
      [—] UNCOMPLETED

DAILY CALLS

(1) [X] [—]   (2) [X] [—]   (3) [X] [—]

(4) [X] [—]   (5) [X] [—]   (6) [X] [—]

(7) [X] [—]   (8) [X] [—]   (9) [X] [—]

(10) [X] [—]   (11) [X] [—]   (12) [X] [—]

(13) [X] [—]   (14) [X] [—]   (15) [X] [—]

"OOPS I FORGOT" - CARRY OVER TOMORROW

TO DO LIST #'S -

DAILY CALL #'S -

DAILY TASKS

DATE:

(1) X —
(2) X —
(3) X —
(4) X —
(5) X —
(6) X —
(7) X —
(8) X —
(9) X —
(10) X —
(11) X —
(12) X —
(13) X —
(14) X —
(15) X —
(16) X —
(17) X —
(18) X —
(19) X —
(20) X —
(21) X —
(22) X —
(23) X —
(24) X —
(25) X —

KEY: ☒ COMPLETED
☐ UNCOMPLETED

DAILY CALLS

① X —   ② X —   ③ X —

④ X —   ⑤ X —   ⑥ X —

⑦ X —   ⑧ X —   ⑨ X —

⑩ X —   ⑪ X —   ⑫ X —

⑬ X —   ⑭ X —   ⑮ X —

"OOPS I FORGOT" - CARRY OVER TOMORROW

TO DO LIST #'S -

DAILY CALL #'S -

DAILY TASKS

DATE:

① X —
② X —
③ X —
④ X —
⑤ X —
⑥ X —
⑦ X —
⑧ X —
⑨ X —
⑩ X —
⑪ X —
⑫ X —
⑬ X —
⑭ X —
⑮ X —
⑯ X —
⑰ X —
⑱ X —
⑲ X —
⑳ X —
㉑ X —
㉒ X —
㉓ X —
㉔ X —
㉕ X —

KEY: ☒ COMPLETED
⊟ UNCOMPLETED

DAILY CALLS

① X —	② X —	③ X —
④ X —	⑤ X —	⑥ X —
⑦ X —	⑧ X —	⑨ X —
⑩ X —	⑪ X —	⑫ X —
⑬ X —	⑭ X —	⑮ X —

"OOPS I FORGOT" - CARRY OVER TOMORROW

TO DO LIST #'S -

DAILY CALL #'S -

DAILY TASKS

DATE:

① X —
② X —
③ X —
④ X —
⑤ X —
⑥ X —
⑦ X —
⑧ X —
⑨ X —
⑩ X —
⑪ X —
⑫ X —
⑬ X —
⑭ X —
⑮ X —
⑯ X —
⑰ X —
⑱ X —
⑲ X —
⑳ X —
㉑ X —
㉒ X —
㉓ X —
㉔ X —
㉕ X —

KEY: ☒ COMPLETED
☒ UNCOMPLETED

DAILY CALLS

① X — 　 ② X — 　 ③ X —

④ X — 　 ⑤ X — 　 ⑥ X —

⑦ X — 　 ⑧ X — 　 ⑨ X —

⑩ X — 　 ⑪ X — 　 ⑫ X —

⑬ X — 　 ⑭ X — 　 ⑮ X —

"OOPS I FORGOT" - CARRY OVER TOMORROW

TO DO LIST #'S -

DAILY CALL #'S -

DAILY TASKS

DATE:

① X —
② X —
③ X —
④ X —
⑤ X —
⑥ X —
⑦ X —
⑧ X —
⑨ X —
⑩ X —
⑪ X —
⑫ X —
⑬ X —
⑭ X —
⑮ X —
⑯ X —
⑰ X —
⑱ X —
⑲ X —
⑳ X —
㉑ X —
㉒ X —
㉓ X —
㉔ X —
㉕ X —

KEY: ☒ COMPLETED
☐ UNCOMPLETED

DAILY CALLS

① X —
② X —
③ X —
④ X —
⑤ X —
⑥ X —
⑦ X —
⑧ X —
⑨ X —
⑩ X —
⑪ X —
⑫ X —
⑬ X —
⑭ X —
⑮ X —

"OOPS I FORGOT" - CARRY OVER TOMORROW

TO DO LIST #'S -

DAILY CALL #'S -

DAILY TASKS

DATE:

① X —
② X —
③ X —
④ X —
⑤ X —
⑥ X —
⑦ X —
⑧ X —
⑨ X —
⑩ X —
⑪ X —
⑫ X —
⑬ X —
⑭ X —
⑮ X —
⑯ X —
⑰ X —
⑱ X —
⑲ X —
⑳ X —
㉑ X —
㉒ X —
㉓ X —
㉔ X —
㉕ X —

KEY: ☒ COMPLETED
☐— UNCOMPLETED

DAILY CALLS

① X —	② X —	③ X —
④ X —	⑤ X —	⑥ X —
⑦ X —	⑧ X —	⑨ X —
⑩ X —	⑪ X —	⑫ X —
⑬ X —	⑭ X —	⑮ X —

"OOPS I FORGOT" - CARRY OVER TOMORROW

TO DO LIST #'S -

DAILY CALL #'S -

DAILY TASKS

DATE:

① X —
② X —
③ X —
④ X —
⑤ X —
⑥ X —
⑦ X —
⑧ X —
⑨ X —
⑩ X —
⑪ X —
⑫ X —
⑬ X —
⑭ X —
⑮ X —
⑯ X —
⑰ X —
⑱ X —
⑲ X —
⑳ X —
㉑ X —
㉒ X —
㉓ X —
㉔ X —
㉕ X —

KEY: ☒ COMPLETED ⊟ UNCOMPLETED

DAILY CALLS

① X ─	② X ─	③ X ─
④ X ─	⑤ X ─	⑥ X ─
⑦ X ─	⑧ X ─	⑨ X ─
⑩ X ─	⑪ X ─	⑫ X ─
⑬ X ─	⑭ X ─	⑮ X ─

"OOPS I FORGOT" - CARRY OVER TOMORROW

TO DO LIST #'S -

DAILY CALL #'S -

DAILY TASKS

DATE:

① X ─
② X ─
③ X ─
④ X ─
⑤ X ─
⑥ X ─
⑦ X ─
⑧ X ─
⑨ X ─
⑩ X ─
⑪ X ─
⑫ X ─
⑬ X ─
⑭ X ─
⑮ X ─
⑯ X ─
⑰ X ─
⑱ X ─
⑲ X ─
⑳ X ─
㉑ X ─
㉒ X ─
㉓ X ─
㉔ X ─
㉕ X ─

KEY: ☒ COMPLETED
      ⊟ UNCOMPLETED

DAILY CALLS

① X ⊟	② X ⊟	③ X ⊟
④ X ⊟	⑤ X ⊟	⑥ X ⊟
⑦ X ⊟	⑧ X ⊟	⑨ X ⊟
⑩ X ⊟	⑪ X ⊟	⑫ X ⊟
⑬ X ⊟	⑭ X ⊟	⑮ X ⊟

"OOPS I FORGOT" - CARRY OVER TOMORROW

TO DO LIST #'S -

DAILY CALL #'S -

DAILY TASKS

DATE:

① X ⊟
② X ⊟
③ X ⊟
④ X ⊟
⑤ X ⊟
⑥ X ⊟
⑦ X ⊟
⑧ X ⊟
⑨ X ⊟
⑩ X ⊟
⑪ X ⊟
⑫ X ⊟
⑬ X ⊟
⑭ X ⊟
⑮ X ⊟
⑯ X ⊟
⑰ X ⊟
⑱ X ⊟
⑲ X ⊟
⑳ X ⊟
㉑ X ⊟
㉒ X ⊟
㉓ X ⊟
㉔ X ⊟
㉕ X ⊟

KEY: ☒ COMPLETED
⊟ UNCOMPLETED

DAILY CALLS

① X —
② X —
③ X —
④ X —
⑤ X —
⑥ X —
⑦ X —
⑧ X —
⑨ X —
⑩ X —
⑪ X —
⑫ X —
⑬ X —
⑭ X —
⑮ X —

"OOPS I FORGOT" - CARRY OVER TOMORROW

TO DO LIST #'S -

DAILY CALL #'S -

DAILY TASKS

DATE:

① X —
② X —
③ X —
④ X —
⑤ X —
⑥ X —
⑦ X —
⑧ X —
⑨ X —
⑩ X —
⑪ X —
⑫ X —
⑬ X —
⑭ X —
⑮ X —
⑯ X —
⑰ X —
⑱ X —
⑲ X —
⑳ X —
㉑ X —
㉒ X —
㉓ X —
㉔ X —
㉕ X —

KEY: ☒ COMPLETED
       ☐ UNCOMPLETED

DAILY CALLS

① ☒ ☐   ② ☒ ☐   ③ ☒ ☐

④ ☒ ☐   ⑤ ☒ ☐   ⑥ ☒ ☐

⑦ ☒ ☐   ⑧ ☒ ☐   ⑨ ☒ ☐

⑩ ☒ ☐   ⑪ ☒ ☐   ⑫ ☒ ☐

⑬ ☒ ☐   ⑭ ☒ ☐   ⑮ ☒ ☐

"OOPS I FORGOT" - CARRY OVER TOMORROW

TO DO LIST #'S -

DAILY CALL #'S -

DAILY TASKS

DATE:

① ☒ ☐
② ☒ ☐
③ ☒ ☐
④ ☒ ☐
⑤ ☒ ☐
⑥ ☒ ☐
⑦ ☒ ☐
⑧ ☒ ☐
⑨ ☒ ☐
⑩ ☒ ☐
⑪ ☒ ☐
⑫ ☒ ☐
⑬ ☒ ☐
⑭ ☒ ☐
⑮ ☒ ☐
⑯ ☒ ☐
⑰ ☒ ☐
⑱ ☒ ☐
⑲ ☒ ☐
⑳ ☒ ☐
㉑ ☒ ☐
㉒ ☒ ☐
㉓ ☒ ☐
㉔ ☒ ☐
㉕ ☒ ☐

KEY: ☒ COMPLETED
☐— UNCOMPLETED

DAILY CALLS

① X —	② X —	③ X —
④ X —	⑤ X —	⑥ X —
⑦ X —	⑧ X —	⑨ X —
⑩ X —	⑪ X —	⑫ X —
⑬ X —	⑭ X —	⑮ X —

"OOPS I FORGOT" - CARRY OVER TOMORROW

TO DO LIST #'S -

DAILY CALL #'S -

DAILY TASKS

DATE:

① X —
② X —
③ X —
④ X —
⑤ X —
⑥ X —
⑦ X —
⑧ X —
⑨ X —
⑩ X —
⑪ X —
⑫ X —
⑬ X —
⑭ X —
⑮ X —
⑯ X —
⑰ X —
⑱ X —
⑲ X —
⑳ X —
㉑ X —
㉒ X —
㉓ X —
㉔ X —
㉕ X —

KEY: [X] COMPLETED
       [—] UNCOMPLETED

DAILY CALLS

① [X] [—]	② [X] [—]	③ [X] [—]
④ [X] [—]	⑤ [X] [—]	⑥ [X] [—]
⑦ [X] [—]	⑧ [X] [—]	⑨ [X] [—]
⑩ [X] [—]	⑪ [X] [—]	⑫ [X] [—]
⑬ [X] [—]	⑭ [X] [—]	⑮ [X] [—]

"OOPS I FORGOT" - CARRY OVER TOMORROW

TO DO LIST #'S -

DAILY CALL #'S -

DAILY TASKS

DATE:

① [X] [—]
② [X] [—]
③ [X] [—]
④ [X] [—]
⑤ [X] [—]
⑥ [X] [—]
⑦ [X] [—]
⑧ [X] [—]
⑨ [X] [—]
⑩ [X] [—]
⑪ [X] [—]
⑫ [X] [—]
⑬ [X] [—]
⑭ [X] [—]
⑮ [X] [—]
⑯ [X] [—]
⑰ [X] [—]
⑱ [X] [—]
⑲ [X] [—]
⑳ [X] [—]
㉑ [X] [—]
㉒ [X] [—]
㉓ [X] [—]
㉔ [X] [—]
㉕ [X] [—]

KEY: ☒ COMPLETED
☐ UNCOMPLETED

DAILY CALLS

① X —   ② X —   ③ X —

④ X —   ⑤ X —   ⑥ X —

⑦ X —   ⑧ X —   ⑨ X —

⑩ X —   ⑪ X —   ⑫ X —

⑬ X —   ⑭ X —   ⑮ X —

"OOPS I FORGOT" - CARRY OVER TOMORROW

TO DO LIST #'S -

DAILY CALL #'S -

DAILY TASKS

DATE:

① X —
② X —
③ X —
④ X —
⑤ X —
⑥ X —
⑦ X —
⑧ X —
⑨ X —
⑩ X —
⑪ X —
⑫ X —
⑬ X —
⑭ X —
⑮ X —
⑯ X —
⑰ X —
⑱ X —
⑲ X —
⑳ X —
㉑ X —
㉒ X —
㉓ X —
㉔ X —
㉕ X —

KEY: ☒ COMPLETED
☐ UNCOMPLETED

DAILY CALLS

① X ─	② X ─	③ X ─
④ X ─	⑤ X ─	⑥ X ─
⑦ X ─	⑧ X ─	⑨ X ─
⑩ X ─	⑪ X ─	⑫ X ─
⑬ X ─	⑭ X ─	⑮ X ─

"OOPS I FORGOT" - CARRY OVER TOMORROW

TO DO LIST #'S -

DAILY CALL #'S -

DAILY TASKS

DATE:

① X ─
② X ─
③ X ─
④ X ─
⑤ X ─
⑥ X ─
⑦ X ─
⑧ X ─
⑨ X ─
⑩ X ─
⑪ X ─
⑫ X ─
⑬ X ─
⑭ X ─
⑮ X ─
⑯ X ─
⑰ X ─
⑱ X ─
⑲ X ─
⑳ X ─
㉑ X ─
㉒ X ─
㉓ X ─
㉔ X ─
㉕ X ─

KEY: ☒ COMPLETED ☐ UNCOMPLETED

DAILY CALLS

① X ☐	② X ☐	③ X ☐
④ X ☐	⑤ X ☐	⑥ X ☐
⑦ X ☐	⑧ X ☐	⑨ X ☐
⑩ X ☐	⑪ X ☐	⑫ X ☐
⑬ X ☐	⑭ X ☐	⑮ X ☐

"OOPS I FORGOT" - CARRY OVER TOMORROW

TO DO LIST #'S -

DAILY CALL #'S -

DAILY TASKS

DATE:

① X ☐
② X ☐
③ X ☐
④ X ☐
⑤ X ☐
⑥ X ☐
⑦ X ☐
⑧ X ☐
⑨ X ☐
⑩ X ☐
⑪ X ☐
⑫ X ☐
⑬ X ☐
⑭ X ☐
⑮ X ☐
⑯ X ☐
⑰ X ☐
⑱ X ☐
⑲ X ☐
⑳ X ☐
㉑ X ☐
㉒ X ☐
㉓ X ☐
㉔ X ☐
㉕ X ☐

KEY: ☒ COMPLETED
⊟ UNCOMPLETED

DAILY CALLS

① ☒ ⊟   ② ☒ ⊟   ③ ☒ ⊟

④ ☒ ⊟   ⑤ ☒ ⊟   ⑥ ☒ ⊟

⑦ ☒ ⊟   ⑧ ☒ ⊟   ⑨ ☒ ⊟

⑩ ☒ ⊟   ⑪ ☒ ⊟   ⑫ ☒ ⊟

⑬ ☒ ⊟   ⑭ ☒ ⊟   ⑮ ☒ ⊟

"OOPS I FORGOT" - CARRY OVER TOMORROW

TO DO LIST #'S -

DAILY CALL #'S -

DAILY TASKS

DATE:

① ☒ ⊟
② ☒ ⊟
③ ☒ ⊟
④ ☒ ⊟
⑤ ☒ ⊟
⑥ ☒ ⊟
⑦ ☒ ⊟
⑧ ☒ ⊟
⑨ ☒ ⊟
⑩ ☒ ⊟
⑪ ☒ ⊟
⑫ ☒ ⊟
⑬ ☒ ⊟
⑭ ☒ ⊟
⑮ ☒ ⊟
⑯ ☒ ⊟
⑰ ☒ ⊟
⑱ ☒ ⊟
⑲ ☒ ⊟
⑳ ☒ ⊟
㉑ ☒ ⊟
㉒ ☒ ⊟
㉓ ☒ ⊟
㉔ ☒ ⊟
㉕ ☒ ⊟

KEY: [X] COMPLETED
      [—] UNCOMPLETED

DAILY CALLS

① [X][—]	② [X][—]	③ [X][—]
④ [X][—]	⑤ [X][—]	⑥ [X][—]
⑦ [X][—]	⑧ [X][—]	⑨ [X][—]
⑩ [X][—]	⑪ [X][—]	⑫ [X][—]
⑬ [X][—]	⑭ [X][—]	⑮ [X][—]

"OOPS I FORGOT" - CARRY OVER TOMORROW

TO DO LIST #'S -

DAILY CALL #'S -

DAILY TASKS

DATE:

① X —
② X —
③ X —
④ X —
⑤ X —
⑥ X —
⑦ X —
⑧ X —
⑨ X —
⑩ X —
⑪ X —
⑫ X —
⑬ X —
⑭ X —
⑮ X —
⑯ X —
⑰ X —
⑱ X —
⑲ X —
⑳ X —
㉑ X —
㉒ X —
㉓ X —
㉔ X —
㉕ X —

KEY: ☒ COMPLETED
☐ UNCOMPLETED

DAILY CALLS

① ☒ ☐   ② ☒ ☐   ③ ☒ ☐

④ ☒ ☐   ⑤ ☒ ☐   ⑥ ☒ ☐

⑦ ☒ ☐   ⑧ ☒ ☐   ⑨ ☒ ☐

⑩ ☒ ☐   ⑪ ☒ ☐   ⑫ ☒ ☐

⑬ ☒ ☐   ⑭ ☒ ☐   ⑮ ☒ ☐

"OOPS I FORGOT" - CARRY OVER TOMORROW

TO DO LIST #'S -

DAILY CALL #'S -

DAILY TASKS

DATE:

① ☒ ☐
② ☒ ☐
③ ☒ ☐
④ ☒ ☐
⑤ ☒ ☐
⑥ ☒ ☐
⑦ ☒ ☐
⑧ ☒ ☐
⑨ ☒ ☐
⑩ ☒ ☐
⑪ ☒ ☐
⑫ ☒ ☐
⑬ ☒ ☐
⑭ ☒ ☐
⑮ ☒ ☐
⑯ ☒ ☐
⑰ ☒ ☐
⑱ ☒ ☐
⑲ ☒ ☐
⑳ ☒ ☐
㉑ ☒ ☐
㉒ ☒ ☐
㉓ ☒ ☐
㉔ ☒ ☐
㉕ ☒ ☐

KEY: [X] COMPLETED [—] UNCOMPLETED

DAILY CALLS

(1) [X] [—]	(2) [X] [—]	(3) [X] [—]
(4) [X] [—]	(5) [X] [—]	(6) [X] [—]
(7) [X] [—]	(8) [X] [—]	(9) [X] [—]
(10) [X] [—]	(11) [X] [—]	(12) [X] [—]
(13) [X] [—]	(14) [X] [—]	(15) [X] [—]

"OOPS I FORGOT" - CARRY OVER TOMORROW

TO DO LIST #'S -

DAILY CALL #'S -

DAILY TASKS

DATE:

(1) [X] [—]
(2) [X] [—]
(3) [X] [—]
(4) [X] [—]
(5) [X] [—]
(6) [X] [—]
(7) [X] [—]
(8) [X] [—]
(9) [X] [—]
(10) [X] [—]
(11) [X] [—]
(12) [X] [—]
(13) [X] [—]
(14) [X] [—]
(15) [X] [—]
(16) [X] [—]
(17) [X] [—]
(18) [X] [—]
(19) [X] [—]
(20) [X] [—]
(21) [X] [—]
(22) [X] [—]
(23) [X] [—]
(24) [X] [—]
(25) [X] [—]

KEY: ☒ COMPLETED
☐ UNCOMPLETED

DAILY CALLS

① ☒ ☐
② ☒ ☐
③ ☒ ☐
④ ☒ ☐
⑤ ☒ ☐
⑥ ☒ ☐
⑦ ☒ ☐
⑧ ☒ ☐
⑨ ☒ ☐
⑩ ☒ ☐
⑪ ☒ ☐
⑫ ☒ ☐
⑬ ☒ ☐
⑭ ☒ ☐
⑮ ☒ ☐

"OOPS I FORGOT" - CARRY OVER TOMORROW

TO DO LIST #'S -

DAILY CALL #'S -

DAILY TASKS

DATE:

① ☒ ☐
② ☒ ☐
③ ☒ ☐
④ ☒ ☐
⑤ ☒ ☐
⑥ ☒ ☐
⑦ ☒ ☐
⑧ ☒ ☐
⑨ ☒ ☐
⑩ ☒ ☐
⑪ ☒ ☐
⑫ ☒ ☐
⑬ ☒ ☐
⑭ ☒ ☐
⑮ ☒ ☐
⑯ ☒ ☐
⑰ ☒ ☐
⑱ ☒ ☐
⑲ ☒ ☐
⑳ ☒ ☐
㉑ ☒ ☐
㉒ ☒ ☐
㉓ ☒ ☐
㉔ ☒ ☐
㉕ ☒ ☐

KEY: ☒ COMPLETED
☐— UNCOMPLETED

DAILY CALLS

① ☒ ☐— ② ☒ ☐— ③ ☒ ☐—

④ ☒ ☐— ⑤ ☒ ☐— ⑥ ☒ ☐—

⑦ ☒ ☐— ⑧ ☒ ☐— ⑨ ☒ ☐—

⑩ ☒ ☐— ⑪ ☒ ☐— ⑫ ☒ ☐—

⑬ ☒ ☐— ⑭ ☒ ☐— ⑮ ☒ ☐—

"OOPS I FORGOT" - CARRY OVER TOMORROW

TO DO LIST #'S -

DAILY CALL #'S -

DAILY TASKS

DATE:

① X —
② X —
③ X —
④ X —
⑤ X —
⑥ X —
⑦ X —
⑧ X —
⑨ X —
⑩ X —
⑪ X —
⑫ X —
⑬ X —
⑭ X —
⑮ X —
⑯ X —
⑰ X —
⑱ X —
⑲ X —
⑳ X —
㉑ X —
㉒ X —
㉓ X —
㉔ X —
㉕ X —

KEY: [X] COMPLETED
      [—] UNCOMPLETED

DAILY CALLS

(1) [X] [—]   (2) [X] [—]   (3) [X] [—]

(4) [X] [—]   (5) [X] [—]   (6) [X] [—]

(7) [X] [—]   (8) [X] [—]   (9) [X] [—]

(10) [X] [—] (11) [X] [—] (12) [X] [—]

(13) [X] [—] (14) [X] [—] (15) [X] [—]

"OOPS I FORGOT" - CARRY OVER TOMORROW

TO DO LIST #'S -

DAILY CALL #'S -

DAILY TASKS

DATE:

(1) X —
(2) X —
(3) X —
(4) X —
(5) X —
(6) X —
(7) X —
(8) X —
(9) X —
(10) X —
(11) X —
(12) X —
(13) X —
(14) X —
(15) X —
(16) X —
(17) X —
(18) X —
(19) X —
(20) X —
(21) X —
(22) X —
(23) X —
(24) X —
(25) X —

KEY: ☒ COMPLETED
⊟ UNCOMPLETED

DAILY CALLS

① X ―	② X ―	③ X ―
④ X ―	⑤ X ―	⑥ X ―
⑦ X ―	⑧ X ―	⑨ X ―
⑩ X ―	⑪ X ―	⑫ X ―
⑬ X ―	⑭ X ―	⑮ X ―

"OOPS I FORGOT" - CARRY OVER TOMORROW

TO DO LIST #'S -

DAILY CALL #'S -

DAILY TASKS
DATE:

① X ―
② X ―
③ X ―
④ X ―
⑤ X ―
⑥ X ―
⑦ X ―
⑧ X ―
⑨ X ―
⑩ X ―
⑪ X ―
⑫ X ―
⑬ X ―
⑭ X ―
⑮ X ―
⑯ X ―
⑰ X ―
⑱ X ―
⑲ X ―
⑳ X ―
㉑ X ―
㉒ X ―
㉓ X ―
㉔ X ―
㉕ X ―

KEY: ☒ COMPLETED
⊟ UNCOMPLETED

DAILY CALLS

① X — ② X — ③ X —

④ X — ⑤ X — ⑥ X —

⑦ X — ⑧ X — ⑨ X —

⑩ X — ⑪ X — ⑫ X —

⑬ X — ⑭ X — ⑮ X —

"OOPS I FORGOT" - CARRY OVER TOMORROW

TO DO LIST #'S -

DAILY CALL #'S -

DAILY TASKS

DATE:

① X —
② X —
③ X —
④ X —
⑤ X —
⑥ X —
⑦ X —
⑧ X —
⑨ X —
⑩ X —
⑪ X —
⑫ X —
⑬ X —
⑭ X —
⑮ X —
⑯ X —
⑰ X —
⑱ X —
⑲ X —
⑳ X —
㉑ X —
㉒ X —
㉓ X —
㉔ X —
㉕ X —

KEY: ☒ COMPLETED
☐— UNCOMPLETED

DAILY CALLS

① X ☐—   ② X ☐—   ③ X ☐—

④ X ☐—   ⑤ X ☐—   ⑥ X ☐—

⑦ X ☐—   ⑧ X ☐—   ⑨ X ☐—

⑩ X ☐—   ⑪ X ☐—   ⑫ X ☐—

⑬ X ☐—   ⑭ X ☐—   ⑮ X ☐—

"OOPS I FORGOT" - CARRY OVER TOMORROW

TO DO LIST #'S -

DAILY CALL #'S -

DAILY TASKS

DATE:

① X —
② X —
③ X —
④ X —
⑤ X —
⑥ X —
⑦ X —
⑧ X —
⑨ X —
⑩ X —
⑪ X —
⑫ X —
⑬ X —
⑭ X —
⑮ X —
⑯ X —
⑰ X —
⑱ X —
⑲ X —
⑳ X —
㉑ X —
㉒ X —
㉓ X —
㉔ X —
㉕ X —

KEY: [X] COMPLETED
[—] UNCOMPLETED

DAILY CALLS

① [X][—]	② [X][—]	③ [X][—]
④ [X][—]	⑤ [X][—]	⑥ [X][—]
⑦ [X][—]	⑧ [X][—]	⑨ [X][—]
⑩ [X][—]	⑪ [X][—]	⑫ [X][—]
⑬ [X][—]	⑭ [X][—]	⑮ [X][—]

"OOPS I FORGOT" - CARRY OVER TOMORROW

TO DO LIST #'S -

DAILY CALL #'S -

DAILY TASKS

DATE:

① X —
② X —
③ X —
④ X —
⑤ X —
⑥ X —
⑦ X —
⑧ X —
⑨ X —
⑩ X —
⑪ X —
⑫ X —
⑬ X —
⑭ X —
⑮ X —
⑯ X —
⑰ X —
⑱ X —
⑲ X —
⑳ X —
㉑ X —
㉒ X —
㉓ X —
㉔ X —
㉕ X —

KEY: [X] COMPLETED
      [—] UNCOMPLETED

DAILY CALLS

(1) [X] [—]	(2) [X] [—]	(3) [X] [—]
(4) [X] [—]	(5) [X] [—]	(6) [X] [—]
(7) [X] [—]	(8) [X] [—]	(9) [X] [—]
(10) [X] [—]	(11) [X] [—]	(12) [X] [—]
(13) [X] [—]	(14) [X] [—]	(15) [X] [—]

"OOPS I FORGOT" - CARRY OVER TOMORROW

TO DO LIST #'S -

DAILY CALL #'S -

DAILY TASKS

DATE:

(1) X —
(2) X —
(3) X —
(4) X —
(5) X —
(6) X —
(7) X —
(8) X —
(9) X —
(10) X —
(11) X —
(12) X —
(13) X —
(14) X —
(15) X —
(16) X —
(17) X —
(18) X —
(19) X —
(20) X —
(21) X —
(22) X —
(23) X —
(24) X —
(25) X —

KEY: ☒ COMPLETED
☐— UNCOMPLETED

DAILY CALLS

① X —
② X —
③ X —
④ X —
⑤ X —
⑥ X —
⑦ X —
⑧ X —
⑨ X —
⑩ X —
⑪ X —
⑫ X —
⑬ X —
⑭ X —
⑮ X —

"OOPS I FORGOT" - CARRY OVER TOMORROW

TO DO LIST #'S -

DAILY CALL #'S -

DAILY TASKS

DATE:

① X —
② X —
③ X —
④ X —
⑤ X —
⑥ X —
⑦ X —
⑧ X —
⑨ X —
⑩ X —
⑪ X —
⑫ X —
⑬ X —
⑭ X —
⑮ X —
⑯ X —
⑰ X —
⑱ X —
⑲ X —
⑳ X —
㉑ X —
㉒ X —
㉓ X —
㉔ X —
㉕ X —

KEY: ☒ COMPLETED
⊟ UNCOMPLETED

DAILY CALLS

① X —	② X —	③ X —
④ X —	⑤ X —	⑥ X —
⑦ X —	⑧ X —	⑨ X —
⑩ X —	⑪ X —	⑫ X —
⑬ X —	⑭ X —	⑮ X —

"OOPS I FORGOT" - CARRY OVER TOMORROW

TO DO LIST #'S -

DAILY CALL #'S -

DAILY TASKS

DATE:

① X —
② X —
③ X —
④ X —
⑤ X —
⑥ X —
⑦ X —
⑧ X —
⑨ X —
⑩ X —
⑪ X —
⑫ X —
⑬ X —
⑭ X —
⑮ X —
⑯ X —
⑰ X —
⑱ X —
⑲ X —
⑳ X —
㉑ X —
㉒ X —
㉓ X —
㉔ X —
㉕ X —

KEY: [X] COMPLETED
      [—] UNCOMPLETED

DAILY CALLS

(1) [X] [—]   (2) [X] [—]   (3) [X] [—]

(4) [X] [—]   (5) [X] [—]   (6) [X] [—]

(7) [X] [—]   (8) [X] [—]   (9) [X] [—]

(10) [X] [—] (11) [X] [—] (12) [X] [—]

(13) [X] [—] (14) [X] [—] (15) [X] [—]

"OOPS I FORGOT" - CARRY OVER TOMORROW

TO DO LIST #'S -

DAILY CALL #'S -

DAILY TASKS

DATE:

(1) [X] [—]
(2) [X] [—]
(3) [X] [—]
(4) [X] [—]
(5) [X] [—]
(6) [X] [—]
(7) [X] [—]
(8) [X] [—]
(9) [X] [—]
(10) [X] [—]
(11) [X] [—]
(12) [X] [—]
(13) [X] [—]
(14) [X] [—]
(15) [X] [—]
(16) [X] [—]
(17) [X] [—]
(18) [X] [—]
(19) [X] [—]
(20) [X] [—]
(21) [X] [—]
(22) [X] [—]
(23) [X] [—]
(24) [X] [—]
(25) [X] [—]

KEY: ☒ COMPLETED
　　　　 ⊟ UNCOMPLETED

DAILY CALLS

(1) X —	(2) X —	(3) X —
(4) X —	(5) X —	(6) X —
(7) X —	(8) X —	(9) X —
(10) X —	(11) X —	(12) X —
(13) X —	(14) X —	(15) X —

"OOPS I FORGOT" - CARRY OVER TOMORROW

TO DO LIST #'S -

DAILY CALL #'S -

DAILY TASKS

DATE:

(1) X —
(2) X —
(3) X —
(4) X —
(5) X —
(6) X —
(7) X —
(8) X —
(9) X —
(10) X —
(11) X —
(12) X —
(13) X —
(14) X —
(15) X —
(16) X —
(17) X —
(18) X —
(19) X —
(20) X —
(21) X —
(22) X —
(23) X —
(24) X —
(25) X —

KEY: ☒ COMPLETED
☐— UNCOMPLETED

DAILY CALLS

① ☒ ☐—
② ☒ ☐—
③ ☒ ☐—
④ ☒ ☐—
⑤ ☒ ☐—
⑥ ☒ ☐—
⑦ ☒ ☐—
⑧ ☒ ☐—
⑨ ☒ ☐—
⑩ ☒ ☐—
⑪ ☒ ☐—
⑫ ☒ ☐—
⑬ ☒ ☐—
⑭ ☒ ☐—
⑮ ☒ ☐—

"OOPS I FORGOT" - CARRY OVER TOMORROW

TO DO LIST #'S -

DAILY CALL #'S -

DAILY TASKS

DATE:

① ☒ ☐—
② ☒ ☐—
③ ☒ ☐—
④ ☒ ☐—
⑤ ☒ ☐—
⑥ ☒ ☐—
⑦ ☒ ☐—
⑧ ☒ ☐—
⑨ ☒ ☐—
⑩ ☒ ☐—
⑪ ☒ ☐—
⑫ ☒ ☐—
⑬ ☒ ☐—
⑭ ☒ ☐—
⑮ ☒ ☐—
⑯ ☒ ☐—
⑰ ☒ ☐—
⑱ ☒ ☐—
⑲ ☒ ☐—
⑳ ☒ ☐—
㉑ ☒ ☐—
㉒ ☒ ☐—
㉓ ☒ ☐—
㉔ ☒ ☐—
㉕ ☒ ☐—

KEY: ☒ COMPLETED
⊟ UNCOMPLETED

DAILY CALLS

(1) X —	(2) X —	(3) X —
(4) X —	(5) X —	(6) X —
(7) X —	(8) X —	(9) X —
(10) X —	(11) X —	(12) X —
(13) X —	(14) X —	(15) X —

"OOPS I FORGOT" - CARRY OVER TOMORROW

TO DO LIST #'S -

DAILY CALL #'S -

DAILY TASKS

DATE:

(1) X —
(2) X —
(3) X —
(4) X —
(5) X —
(6) X —
(7) X —
(8) X —
(9) X —
(10) X —
(11) X —
(12) X —
(13) X —
(14) X —
(15) X —
(16) X —
(17) X —
(18) X —
(19) X —
(20) X —
(21) X —
(22) X —
(23) X —
(24) X —
(25) X —

KEY: ☒ COMPLETED
       ⊟ UNCOMPLETED

DAILY CALLS

① X ⊟	② X ⊟	③ X ⊟
④ X ⊟	⑤ X ⊟	⑥ X ⊟
⑦ X ⊟	⑧ X ⊟	⑨ X ⊟
⑩ X ⊟	⑪ X ⊟	⑫ X ⊟
⑬ X ⊟	⑭ X ⊟	⑮ X ⊟

"OOPS I FORGOT" - CARRY OVER TOMORROW

TO DO LIST #'S -

DAILY CALL #'S -

DAILY TASKS

DATE:

① X ⊟
② X ⊟
③ X ⊟
④ X ⊟
⑤ X ⊟
⑥ X ⊟
⑦ X ⊟
⑧ X ⊟
⑨ X ⊟
⑩ X ⊟
⑪ X ⊟
⑫ X ⊟
⑬ X ⊟
⑭ X ⊟
⑮ X ⊟
⑯ X ⊟
⑰ X ⊟
⑱ X ⊟
⑲ X ⊟
⑳ X ⊟
㉑ X ⊟
㉒ X ⊟
㉓ X ⊟
㉔ X ⊟
㉕ X ⊟

KEY: ☒ COMPLETED ☐ UNCOMPLETED

DAILY CALLS

① X —	② X —	③ X —
④ X —	⑤ X —	⑥ X —
⑦ X —	⑧ X —	⑨ X —
⑩ X —	⑪ X —	⑫ X —
⑬ X —	⑭ X —	⑮ X —

"OOPS I FORGOT" - CARRY OVER TOMORROW

TO DO LIST #'S -

DAILY CALL #'S -

DAILY TASKS

DATE:

① X —
② X —
③ X —
④ X —
⑤ X —
⑥ X —
⑦ X —
⑧ X —
⑨ X —
⑩ X —
⑪ X —
⑫ X —
⑬ X —
⑭ X —
⑮ X —
⑯ X —
⑰ X —
⑱ X —
⑲ X —
⑳ X —
㉑ X —
㉒ X —
㉓ X —
㉔ X —
㉕ X —

KEY: ☒ COMPLETED
⊟ UNCOMPLETED

DAILY CALLS

① X —
② X —
③ X —
④ X —
⑤ X —
⑥ X —
⑦ X —
⑧ X —
⑨ X —
⑩ X —
⑪ X —
⑫ X —
⑬ X —
⑭ X —
⑮ X —

"OOPS I FORGOT" - CARRY OVER TOMORROW

TO DO LIST #'S -

DAILY CALL #'S -

DAILY TASKS

DATE:

① X —
② X —
③ X —
④ X —
⑤ X —
⑥ X —
⑦ X —
⑧ X —
⑨ X —
⑩ X —
⑪ X —
⑫ X —
⑬ X —
⑭ X —
⑮ X —
⑯ X —
⑰ X —
⑱ X —
⑲ X —
⑳ X —
㉑ X —
㉒ X —
㉓ X —
㉔ X —
㉕ X —

KEY: ☒ COMPLETED
☐— UNCOMPLETED

DAILY CALLS

(1) X —	(2) X —	(3) X —
(4) X —	(5) X —	(6) X —
(7) X —	(8) X —	(9) X —
(10) X —	(11) X —	(12) X —
(13) X —	(14) X —	(15) X —

"OOPS I FORGOT" - CARRY OVER TOMORROW

TO DO LIST #'S -

DAILY CALL #'S -

DAILY TASKS

DATE:

(1) X —
(2) X —
(3) X —
(4) X —
(5) X —
(6) X —
(7) X —
(8) X —
(9) X —
(10) X —
(11) X —
(12) X —
(13) X —
(14) X —
(15) X —
(16) X —
(17) X —
(18) X —
(19) X —
(20) X —
(21) X —
(22) X —
(23) X —
(24) X —
(25) X —

KEY: ☒ COMPLETED
      ⊟ UNCOMPLETED

DAILY CALLS

① X —	② X —	③ X —
④ X —	⑤ X —	⑥ X —
⑦ X —	⑧ X —	⑨ X —
⑩ X —	⑪ X —	⑫ X —
⑬ X —	⑭ X —	⑮ X —

"OOPS I FORGOT" - CARRY OVER TOMORROW

TO DO LIST #'S -

DAILY CALL #'S -

DAILY TASKS

DATE:

① X —
② X —
③ X —
④ X —
⑤ X —
⑥ X —
⑦ X —
⑧ X —
⑨ X —
⑩ X —
⑪ X —
⑫ X —
⑬ X —
⑭ X —
⑮ X —
⑯ X —
⑰ X —
⑱ X —
⑲ X —
⑳ X —
㉑ X —
㉒ X —
㉓ X —
㉔ X —
㉕ X —

KEY: ☒ COMPLETED
☐− UNCOMPLETED

DAILY CALLS

① ☒ ☐−   ② ☒ ☐−   ③ ☒ ☐−

④ ☒ ☐−   ⑤ ☒ ☐−   ⑥ ☒ ☐−

⑦ ☒ ☐−   ⑧ ☒ ☐−   ⑨ ☒ ☐−

⑩ ☒ ☐−   ⑪ ☒ ☐−   ⑫ ☒ ☐−

⑬ ☒ ☐−   ⑭ ☒ ☐−   ⑮ ☒ ☐−

"OOPS I FORGOT" - CARRY OVER TOMORROW

TO DO LIST #'S -

DAILY CALL #'S -

DAILY TASKS

DATE:

① X −
② X −
③ X −
④ X −
⑤ X −
⑥ X −
⑦ X −
⑧ X −
⑨ X −
⑩ X −
⑪ X −
⑫ X −
⑬ X −
⑭ X −
⑮ X −
⑯ X −
⑰ X −
⑱ X −
⑲ X −
⑳ X −
㉑ X −
㉒ X −
㉓ X −
㉔ X −
㉕ X −

KEY: ☒ COMPLETED
☐ UNCOMPLETED

DAILY CALLS

① X —	② X —	③ X —
④ X —	⑤ X —	⑥ X —
⑦ X —	⑧ X —	⑨ X —
⑩ X —	⑪ X —	⑫ X —
⑬ X —	⑭ X —	⑮ X —

"OOPS I FORGOT" - CARRY OVER TOMORROW

TO DO LIST #'S -

DAILY CALL #'S -

DAILY TASKS
DATE:

① X —
② X —
③ X —
④ X —
⑤ X —
⑥ X —
⑦ X —
⑧ X —
⑨ X —
⑩ X —
⑪ X —
⑫ X —
⑬ X —
⑭ X —
⑮ X —
⑯ X —
⑰ X —
⑱ X —
⑲ X —
⑳ X —
㉑ X —
㉒ X —
㉓ X —
㉔ X —
㉕ X —

KEY: ☒ COMPLETED
☐ UNCOMPLETED

DAILY CALLS

① X ─	② X ─	③ X ─
④ X ─	⑤ X ─	⑥ X ─
⑦ X ─	⑧ X ─	⑨ X ─
⑩ X ─	⑪ X ─	⑫ X ─
⑬ X ─	⑭ X ─	⑮ X ─

"OOPS I FORGOT" - CARRY OVER TOMORROW

TO DO LIST #'S -

DAILY CALL #'S -

DAILY TASKS

DATE:

① X ─
② X ─
③ X ─
④ X ─
⑤ X ─
⑥ X ─
⑦ X ─
⑧ X ─
⑨ X ─
⑩ X ─
⑪ X ─
⑫ X ─
⑬ X ─
⑭ X ─
⑮ X ─
⑯ X ─
⑰ X ─
⑱ X ─
⑲ X ─
⑳ X ─
㉑ X ─
㉒ X ─
㉓ X ─
㉔ X ─
㉕ X ─

KEY: ☒ COMPLETED
      ⊟ UNCOMPLETED

DAILY CALLS

① X — ② X — ③ X —

④ X — ⑤ X — ⑥ X —

⑦ X — ⑧ X — ⑨ X —

⑩ X — ⑪ X — ⑫ X —

⑬ X — ⑭ X — ⑮ X —

"OOPS I FORGOT" - CARRY OVER TOMORROW

TO DO LIST #'S -

DAILY CALL #'S -

DAILY TASKS

DATE:

① X —
② X —
③ X —
④ X —
⑤ X —
⑥ X —
⑦ X —
⑧ X —
⑨ X —
⑩ X —
⑪ X —
⑫ X —
⑬ X —
⑭ X —
⑮ X —
⑯ X —
⑰ X —
⑱ X —
⑲ X —
⑳ X —
㉑ X —
㉒ X —
㉓ X —
㉔ X —
㉕ X —

KEY: ☒ COMPLETED
⊟ UNCOMPLETED

DAILY CALLS

(1) X — (2) X — (3) X —

(4) X — (5) X — (6) X —

(7) X — (8) X — (9) X —

(10) X — (11) X — (12) X —

(13) X — (14) X — (15) X —

"OOPS I FORGOT" - CARRY OVER TOMORROW

TO DO LIST #'S -

DAILY CALL #'S -

DAILY TASKS
DATE:

(1) X —
(2) X —
(3) X —
(4) X —
(5) X —
(6) X —
(7) X —
(8) X —
(9) X —
(10) X —
(11) X —
(12) X —
(13) X —
(14) X —
(15) X —
(16) X —
(17) X —
(18) X —
(19) X —
(20) X —
(21) X —
(22) X —
(23) X —
(24) X —
(25) X —

KEY: ☒ COMPLETED
⊟ UNCOMPLETED

DAILY CALLS

① X — ② X — ③ X —

④ X — ⑤ X — ⑥ X —

⑦ X — ⑧ X — ⑨ X —

⑩ X — ⑪ X — ⑫ X —

⑬ X — ⑭ X — ⑮ X —

"OOPS I FORGOT" - CARRY OVER TOMORROW

TO DO LIST #'S -

DAILY CALL #'S -

DAILY TASKS

DATE:

① X —
② X —
③ X —
④ X —
⑤ X —
⑥ X —
⑦ X —
⑧ X —
⑨ X —
⑩ X —
⑪ X —
⑫ X —
⑬ X —
⑭ X —
⑮ X —
⑯ X —
⑰ X —
⑱ X —
⑲ X —
⑳ X —
㉑ X —
㉒ X —
㉓ X —
㉔ X —
㉕ X —

KEY: ☒ COMPLETED
⊟ UNCOMPLETED

DAILY CALLS

1 X —	2 X —	3 X —
4 X —	5 X —	6 X —
7 X —	8 X —	9 X —
10 X —	11 X —	12 X —
13 X —	14 X —	15 X —

"OOPS I FORGOT" - CARRY OVER TOMORROW

TO DO LIST #'S -

DAILY CALL #'S -

DAILY TASKS

DATE:

1. X —
2. X —
3. X —
4. X —
5. X —
6. X —
7. X —
8. X —
9. X —
10. X —
11. X —
12. X —
13. X —
14. X —
15. X —
16. X —
17. X —
18. X —
19. X —
20. X —
21. X —
22. X —
23. X —
24. X —
25. X —

KEY: ☒ COMPLETED
☐– UNCOMPLETED

DAILY CALLS

① ☒ ☐–   ② ☒ ☐–   ③ ☒ ☐–

④ ☒ ☐–   ⑤ ☒ ☐–   ⑥ ☒ ☐–

⑦ ☒ ☐–   ⑧ ☒ ☐–   ⑨ ☒ ☐–

⑩ ☒ ☐–   ⑪ ☒ ☐–   ⑫ ☒ ☐–

⑬ ☒ ☐–   ⑭ ☒ ☐–   ⑮ ☒ ☐–

"OOPS I FORGOT" - CARRY OVER TOMORROW

TO DO LIST #'S -

DAILY CALL #'S -

DAILY TASKS

DATE:

① X –
② X –
③ X –
④ X –
⑤ X –
⑥ X –
⑦ X –
⑧ X –
⑨ X –
⑩ X –
⑪ X –
⑫ X –
⑬ X –
⑭ X –
⑮ X –
⑯ X –
⑰ X –
⑱ X –
⑲ X –
⑳ X –
㉑ X –
㉒ X –
㉓ X –
㉔ X –
㉕ X –

KEY: ☒ COMPLETED
⊟ UNCOMPLETED

DAILY CALLS

① X ⊟	② X ⊟	③ X ⊟
④ X ⊟	⑤ X ⊟	⑥ X ⊟
⑦ X ⊟	⑧ X ⊟	⑨ X ⊟
⑩ X ⊟	⑪ X ⊟	⑫ X ⊟
⑬ X ⊟	⑭ X ⊟	⑮ X ⊟

"OOPS I FORGOT" - CARRY OVER TOMORROW

TO DO LIST #'S -

DAILY CALL #'S -

DAILY TASKS

DATE:

① X ⊟
② X ⊟
③ X ⊟
④ X ⊟
⑤ X ⊟
⑥ X ⊟
⑦ X ⊟
⑧ X ⊟
⑨ X ⊟
⑩ X ⊟
⑪ X ⊟
⑫ X ⊟
⑬ X ⊟
⑭ X ⊟
⑮ X ⊟
⑯ X ⊟
⑰ X ⊟
⑱ X ⊟
⑲ X ⊟
⑳ X ⊟
㉑ X ⊟
㉒ X ⊟
㉓ X ⊟
㉔ X ⊟
㉕ X ⊟

KEY: ☒ COMPLETED
☐— UNCOMPLETED

DAILY CALLS

① X —	② X —	③ X —
④ X —	⑤ X —	⑥ X —
⑦ X —	⑧ X —	⑨ X —
⑩ X —	⑪ X —	⑫ X —
⑬ X —	⑭ X —	⑮ X —

"OOPS I FORGOT" - CARRY OVER TOMORROW

TO DO LIST #'S -

DAILY CALL #'S -

DAILY TASKS
DATE:

① X —
② X —
③ X —
④ X —
⑤ X —
⑥ X —
⑦ X —
⑧ X —
⑨ X —
⑩ X —
⑪ X —
⑫ X —
⑬ X —
⑭ X —
⑮ X —
⑯ X —
⑰ X —
⑱ X —
⑲ X —
⑳ X —
㉑ X —
㉒ X —
㉓ X —
㉔ X —
㉕ X —

KEY: ☒ COMPLETED
☐— UNCOMPLETED

DAILY CALLS

(1) ☒ ☐—	(2) ☒ ☐—	(3) ☒ ☐—
(4) ☒ ☐—	(5) ☒ ☐—	(6) ☒ ☐—
(7) ☒ ☐—	(8) ☒ ☐—	(9) ☒ ☐—
(10) ☒ ☐—	(11) ☒ ☐—	(12) ☒ ☐—
(13) ☒ ☐—	(14) ☒ ☐—	(15) ☒ ☐—

"OOPS I FORGOT" - CARRY OVER TOMORROW

TO DO LIST #'S -

DAILY CALL #'S -

DAILY TASKS

DATE:

1. ☒ ☐—
2. ☒ ☐—
3. ☒ ☐—
4. ☒ ☐—
5. ☒ ☐—
6. ☒ ☐—
7. ☒ ☐—
8. ☒ ☐—
9. ☒ ☐—
10. ☒ ☐—
11. ☒ ☐—
12. ☒ ☐—
13. ☒ ☐—
14. ☒ ☐—
15. ☒ ☐—
16. ☒ ☐—
17. ☒ ☐—
18. ☒ ☐—
19. ☒ ☐—
20. ☒ ☐—
21. ☒ ☐—
22. ☒ ☐—
23. ☒ ☐—
24. ☒ ☐—
25. ☒ ☐—

KEY: [X] COMPLETED
      [—] UNCOMPLETED

DAILY CALLS

(1) [X][—]
(2) [X][—]
(3) [X][—]
(4) [X][—]
(5) [X][—]
(6) [X][—]
(7) [X][—]
(8) [X][—]
(9) [X][—]
(10) [X][—]
(11) [X][—]
(12) [X][—]
(13) [X][—]
(14) [X][—]
(15) [X][—]

"OOPS I FORGOT" - CARRY OVER TOMORROW

TO DO LIST #'S -

DAILY CALL #'S -

DAILY TASKS

DATE:

(1) X —
(2) X —
(3) X —
(4) X —
(5) X —
(6) X —
(7) X —
(8) X —
(9) X —
(10) X —
(11) X —
(12) X —
(13) X —
(14) X —
(15) X —
(16) X —
(17) X —
(18) X —
(19) X —
(20) X —
(21) X —
(22) X —
(23) X —
(24) X —
(25) X —

KEY: [X] COMPLETED [—] UNCOMPLETED

DAILY CALLS

(1) [X] [—]
(2) [X] [—]
(3) [X] [—]
(4) [X] [—]
(5) [X] [—]
(6) [X] [—]
(7) [X] [—]
(8) [X] [—]
(9) [X] [—]
(10) [X] [—]
(11) [X] [—]
(12) [X] [—]
(13) [X] [—]
(14) [X] [—]
(15) [X] [—]

"OOPS I FORGOT" - CARRY OVER TOMORROW

TO DO LIST #'S -

DAILY CALL #'S -

DAILY TASKS

DATE:

(1) [X] [—]
(2) [X] [—]
(3) [X] [—]
(4) [X] [—]
(5) [X] [—]
(6) [X] [—]
(7) [X] [—]
(8) [X] [—]
(9) [X] [—]
(10) [X] [—]
(11) [X] [—]
(12) [X] [—]
(13) [X] [—]
(14) [X] [—]
(15) [X] [—]
(16) [X] [—]
(17) [X] [—]
(18) [X] [—]
(19) [X] [—]
(20) [X] [—]
(21) [X] [—]
(22) [X] [—]
(23) [X] [—]
(24) [X] [—]
(25) [X] [—]

KEY: ☒ COMPLETED
☐ UNCOMPLETED

DAILY CALLS

① X ─	② X ─	③ X ─
④ X ─	⑤ X ─	⑥ X ─
⑦ X ─	⑧ X ─	⑨ X ─
⑩ X ─	⑪ X ─	⑫ X ─
⑬ X ─	⑭ X ─	⑮ X ─

"OOPS I FORGOT" - CARRY OVER TOMORROW

TO DO LIST #'S -

DAILY CALL #'S -

DAILY TASKS

DATE:

① X ─
② X ─
③ X ─
④ X ─
⑤ X ─
⑥ X ─
⑦ X ─
⑧ X ─
⑨ X ─
⑩ X ─
⑪ X ─
⑫ X ─
⑬ X ─
⑭ X ─
⑮ X ─
⑯ X ─
⑰ X ─
⑱ X ─
⑲ X ─
⑳ X ─
㉑ X ─
㉒ X ─
㉓ X ─
㉔ X ─
㉕ X ─

KEY: ☒ COMPLETED
☐− UNCOMPLETED

DAILY CALLS

① X − 　② X − 　③ X −

④ X − 　⑤ X − 　⑥ X −

⑦ X − 　⑧ X − 　⑨ X −

⑩ X − 　⑪ X − 　⑫ X −

⑬ X − 　⑭ X − 　⑮ X −

"OOPS I FORGOT" - CARRY OVER TOMORROW

TO DO LIST #'S -

DAILY CALL #'S -

DAILY TASKS

DATE:

① X −
② X −
③ X −
④ X −
⑤ X −
⑥ X −
⑦ X −
⑧ X −
⑨ X −
⑩ X −
⑪ X −
⑫ X −
⑬ X −
⑭ X −
⑮ X −
⑯ X −
⑰ X −
⑱ X −
⑲ X −
⑳ X −
㉑ X −
㉒ X −
㉓ X −
㉔ X −
㉕ X −

KEY: ☒ COMPLETED
      ☐− UNCOMPLETED

DAILY CALLS

① X −   ② X −   ③ X −

④ X −   ⑤ X −   ⑥ X −

⑦ X −   ⑧ X −   ⑨ X −

⑩ X −   ⑪ X −   ⑫ X −

⑬ X −   ⑭ X −   ⑮ X −

"OOPS I FORGOT" - CARRY OVER TOMORROW

TO DO LIST #'S -

DAILY CALL #'S -

DAILY TASKS

DATE:

① X −
② X −
③ X −
④ X −
⑤ X −
⑥ X −
⑦ X −
⑧ X −
⑨ X −
⑩ X −
⑪ X −
⑫ X −
⑬ X −
⑭ X −
⑮ X −
⑯ X −
⑰ X −
⑱ X −
⑲ X −
⑳ X −
㉑ X −
㉒ X −
㉓ X −
㉔ X −
㉕ X −

KEY: ☒ COMPLETED
☐— UNCOMPLETED

DAILY CALLS

① X — ② X — ③ X —

④ X — ⑤ X — ⑥ X —

⑦ X — ⑧ X — ⑨ X —

⑩ X — ⑪ X — ⑫ X —

⑬ X — ⑭ X — ⑮ X —

"OOPS I FORGOT" - CARRY OVER TOMORROW

TO DO LIST #'S -

DAILY CALL #'S -

DAILY TASKS

DATE:

① X —
② X —
③ X —
④ X —
⑤ X —
⑥ X —
⑦ X —
⑧ X —
⑨ X —
⑩ X —
⑪ X —
⑫ X —
⑬ X —
⑭ X —
⑮ X —
⑯ X —
⑰ X —
⑱ X —
⑲ X —
⑳ X —
㉑ X —
㉒ X —
㉓ X —
㉔ X —
㉕ X —

KEY: ☒ COMPLETED
⊟ UNCOMPLETED

DAILY CALLS

① X —
② X —
③ X —
④ X —
⑤ X —
⑥ X —
⑦ X —
⑧ X —
⑨ X —
⑩ X —
⑪ X —
⑫ X —
⑬ X —
⑭ X —
⑮ X —

"OOPS I FORGOT" - CARRY OVER TOMORROW

TO DO LIST #'S -

DAILY CALL #'S -

DAILY TASKS

DATE:

① X —
② X —
③ X —
④ X —
⑤ X —
⑥ X —
⑦ X —
⑧ X —
⑨ X —
⑩ X —
⑪ X —
⑫ X —
⑬ X —
⑭ X —
⑮ X —
⑯ X —
⑰ X —
⑱ X —
⑲ X —
⑳ X —
㉑ X —
㉒ X —
㉓ X —
㉔ X —
㉕ X —

KEY: [X] COMPLETED
[—] UNCOMPLETED

DAILY CALLS

(1) [X] [—]
(2) [X] [—]
(3) [X] [—]

(4) [X] [—]
(5) [X] [—]
(6) [X] [—]

(7) [X] [—]
(8) [X] [—]
(9) [X] [—]

(10) [X] [—]
(11) [X] [—]
(12) [X] [—]

(13) [X] [—]
(14) [X] [—]
(15) [X] [—]

"OOPS I FORGOT" - CARRY OVER TOMORROW

TO DO LIST #'S -

DAILY CALL #'S -

DAILY TASKS

DATE:

(1) [X] [—]
(2) [X] [—]
(3) [X] [—]
(4) [X] [—]
(5) [X] [—]
(6) [X] [—]
(7) [X] [—]
(8) [X] [—]
(9) [X] [—]
(10) [X] [—]
(11) [X] [—]
(12) [X] [—]
(13) [X] [—]
(14) [X] [—]
(15) [X] [—]
(16) [X] [—]
(17) [X] [—]
(18) [X] [—]
(19) [X] [—]
(20) [X] [—]
(21) [X] [—]
(22) [X] [—]
(23) [X] [—]
(24) [X] [—]
(25) [X] [—]

KEY: [X] COMPLETED
       [—] UNCOMPLETED

DAILY CALLS

① [X][—]   ② [X][—]   ③ [X][—]

④ [X][—]   ⑤ [X][—]   ⑥ [X][—]

⑦ [X][—]   ⑧ [X][—]   ⑨ [X][—]

⑩ [X][—]   ⑪ [X][—]   ⑫ [X][—]

⑬ [X][—]   ⑭ [X][—]   ⑮ [X][—]

"OOPS I FORGOT" - CARRY OVER TOMORROW

TO DO LIST #'S -

DAILY CALL #'S -

DAILY TASKS

DATE:

① [X][—]
② [X][—]
③ [X][—]
④ [X][—]
⑤ [X][—]
⑥ [X][—]
⑦ [X][—]
⑧ [X][—]
⑨ [X][—]
⑩ [X][—]
⑪ [X][—]
⑫ [X][—]
⑬ [X][—]
⑭ [X][—]
⑮ [X][—]
⑯ [X][—]
⑰ [X][—]
⑱ [X][—]
⑲ [X][—]
⑳ [X][—]
㉑ [X][—]
㉒ [X][—]
㉓ [X][—]
㉔ [X][—]
㉕ [X][—]

KEY: ☒ COMPLETED
☐ UNCOMPLETED

DAILY CALLS

① X ─   ② X ─   ③ X ─

④ X ─   ⑤ X ─   ⑥ X ─

⑦ X ─   ⑧ X ─   ⑨ X ─

⑩ X ─   ⑪ X ─   ⑫ X ─

⑬ X ─   ⑭ X ─   ⑮ X ─

"OOPS I FORGOT" - CARRY OVER TOMORROW

TO DO LIST #'S -

DAILY CALL #'S -

DAILY TASKS

DATE:

① X ─
② X ─
③ X ─
④ X ─
⑤ X ─
⑥ X ─
⑦ X ─
⑧ X ─
⑨ X ─
⑩ X ─
⑪ X ─
⑫ X ─
⑬ X ─
⑭ X ─
⑮ X ─
⑯ X ─
⑰ X ─
⑱ X ─
⑲ X ─
⑳ X ─
㉑ X ─
㉒ X ─
㉓ X ─
㉔ X ─
㉕ X ─

KEY: ☒ COMPLETED
☐ UNCOMPLETED

DAILY CALLS

① X ─	② X ─	③ X ─
④ X ─	⑤ X ─	⑥ X ─
⑦ X ─	⑧ X ─	⑨ X ─
⑩ X ─	⑪ X ─	⑫ X ─
⑬ X ─	⑭ X ─	⑮ X ─

"OOPS I FORGOT" - CARRY OVER TOMORROW

TO DO LIST #'S -

DAILY CALL #'S -

DAILY TASKS

DATE:

① X ─
② X ─
③ X ─
④ X ─
⑤ X ─
⑥ X ─
⑦ X ─
⑧ X ─
⑨ X ─
⑩ X ─
⑪ X ─
⑫ X ─
⑬ X ─
⑭ X ─
⑮ X ─
⑯ X ─
⑰ X ─
⑱ X ─
⑲ X ─
⑳ X ─
㉑ X ─
㉒ X ─
㉓ X ─
㉔ X ─
㉕ X ─

KEY: ☒ COMPLETED
      ☐ UNCOMPLETED

DAILY CALLS

① X —   ② X —   ③ X —

④ X —   ⑤ X —   ⑥ X —

⑦ X —   ⑧ X —   ⑨ X —

⑩ X —   ⑪ X —   ⑫ X —

⑬ X —   ⑭ X —   ⑮ X —

"OOPS I FORGOT" - CARRY OVER TOMORROW

TO DO LIST #'S -

DAILY CALL #'S -

DAILY TASKS

DATE:

① X —
② X —
③ X —
④ X —
⑤ X —
⑥ X —
⑦ X —
⑧ X —
⑨ X —
⑩ X —
⑪ X —
⑫ X —
⑬ X —
⑭ X —
⑮ X —
⑯ X —
⑰ X —
⑱ X —
⑲ X —
⑳ X —
㉑ X —
㉒ X —
㉓ X —
㉔ X —
㉕ X —

KEY: ☒ COMPLETED
⊟ UNCOMPLETED

DAILY CALLS

① X —
② X —
③ X —
④ X —
⑤ X —
⑥ X —
⑦ X —
⑧ X —
⑨ X —
⑩ X —
⑪ X —
⑫ X —
⑬ X —
⑭ X —
⑮ X —

"OOPS I FORGOT" - CARRY OVER TOMORROW

TO DO LIST #'S -

DAILY CALL #'S -

DAILY TASKS

DATE:

① X —
② X —
③ X —
④ X —
⑤ X —
⑥ X —
⑦ X —
⑧ X —
⑨ X —
⑩ X —
⑪ X —
⑫ X —
⑬ X —
⑭ X —
⑮ X —
⑯ X —
⑰ X —
⑱ X —
⑲ X —
⑳ X —
㉑ X —
㉒ X —
㉓ X —
㉔ X —
㉕ X —

KEY: ☒ COMPLETED
☐ UNCOMPLETED

DAILY CALLS

① X —
② X —
③ X —
④ X —
⑤ X —
⑥ X —
⑦ X —
⑧ X —
⑨ X —
⑩ X —
⑪ X —
⑫ X —
⑬ X —
⑭ X —
⑮ X —

"OOPS I FORGOT" - CARRY OVER TOMORROW

TO DO LIST #'S -

DAILY CALL #'S -

DAILY TASKS

DATE:

① X —
② X —
③ X —
④ X —
⑤ X —
⑥ X —
⑦ X —
⑧ X —
⑨ X —
⑩ X —
⑪ X —
⑫ X —
⑬ X —
⑭ X —
⑮ X —
⑯ X —
⑰ X —
⑱ X —
⑲ X —
⑳ X —
㉑ X —
㉒ X —
㉓ X —
㉔ X —
㉕ X —

KEY: ☒ COMPLETED
☐ UNCOMPLETED

DAILY CALLS

① X — ② X — ③ X —

④ X — ⑤ X — ⑥ X —

⑦ X — ⑧ X — ⑨ X —

⑩ X — ⑪ X — ⑫ X —

⑬ X — ⑭ X — ⑮ X —

"OOPS I FORGOT" - CARRY OVER TOMORROW

TO DO LIST #'S -

DAILY CALL #'S -

DAILY TASKS

DATE:

① X —
② X —
③ X —
④ X —
⑤ X —
⑥ X —
⑦ X —
⑧ X —
⑨ X —
⑩ X —
⑪ X —
⑫ X —
⑬ X —
⑭ X —
⑮ X —
⑯ X —
⑰ X —
⑱ X —
⑲ X —
⑳ X —
㉑ X —
㉒ X —
㉓ X —
㉔ X —
㉕ X —

KEY: ☒ COMPLETED
⊟ UNCOMPLETED

DAILY CALLS

① X —	② X —	③ X —
④ X —	⑤ X —	⑥ X —
⑦ X —	⑧ X —	⑨ X —
⑩ X —	⑪ X —	⑫ X —
⑬ X —	⑭ X —	⑮ X —

"OOPS I FORGOT" - CARRY OVER TOMORROW

TO DO LIST #'S -

DAILY CALL #'S -

DAILY TASKS

DATE:

① X —
② X —
③ X —
④ X —
⑤ X —
⑥ X —
⑦ X —
⑧ X —
⑨ X —
⑩ X —
⑪ X —
⑫ X —
⑬ X —
⑭ X —
⑮ X —
⑯ X —
⑰ X —
⑱ X —
⑲ X —
⑳ X —
㉑ X —
㉒ X —
㉓ X —
㉔ X —
㉕ X —

KEY: ☒ COMPLETED
☐ UNCOMPLETED

DAILY CALLS

① X ─	② X ─	③ X ─
④ X ─	⑤ X ─	⑥ X ─
⑦ X ─	⑧ X ─	⑨ X ─
⑩ X ─	⑪ X ─	⑫ X ─
⑬ X ─	⑭ X ─	⑮ X ─

"OOPS I FORGOT" - CARRY OVER TOMORROW

TO DO LIST #'S -

DAILY CALL #'S -

DAILY TASKS

DATE:

① X ─
② X ─
③ X ─
④ X ─
⑤ X ─
⑥ X ─
⑦ X ─
⑧ X ─
⑨ X ─
⑩ X ─
⑪ X ─
⑫ X ─
⑬ X ─
⑭ X ─
⑮ X ─
⑯ X ─
⑰ X ─
⑱ X ─
⑲ X ─
⑳ X ─
㉑ X ─
㉒ X ─
㉓ X ─
㉔ X ─
㉕ X ─

KEY: [X] COMPLETED
[—] UNCOMPLETED

DAILY CALLS

(1) [X] [—]   (2) [X] [—]   (3) [X] [—]

(4) [X] [—]   (5) [X] [—]   (6) [X] [—]

(7) [X] [—]   (8) [X] [—]   (9) [X] [—]

(10) [X] [—]   (11) [X] [—]   (12) [X] [—]

(13) [X] [—]   (14) [X] [—]   (15) [X] [—]

"OOPS I FORGOT" - CARRY OVER TOMORROW

TO DO LIST #'S -

DAILY CALL #'S -

DAILY TASKS

DATE:

(1) X —
(2) X —
(3) X —
(4) X —
(5) X —
(6) X —
(7) X —
(8) X —
(9) X —
(10) X —
(11) X —
(12) X —
(13) X —
(14) X —
(15) X —
(16) X —
(17) X —
(18) X —
(19) X —
(20) X —
(21) X —
(22) X —
(23) X —
(24) X —
(25) X —

KEY: ☒ COMPLETED
☐− UNCOMPLETED

DAILY CALLS

① X −	② X −	③ X −
④ X −	⑤ X −	⑥ X −
⑦ X −	⑧ X −	⑨ X −
⑩ X −	⑪ X −	⑫ X −
⑬ X −	⑭ X −	⑮ X −

"OOPS I FORGOT" - CARRY OVER TOMORROW

TO DO LIST #'S -

DAILY CALL #'S -

DAILY TASKS

DATE:

① X −
② X −
③ X −
④ X −
⑤ X −
⑥ X −
⑦ X −
⑧ X −
⑨ X −
⑩ X −
⑪ X −
⑫ X −
⑬ X −
⑭ X −
⑮ X −
⑯ X −
⑰ X −
⑱ X −
⑲ X −
⑳ X −
㉑ X −
㉒ X −
㉓ X −
㉔ X −
㉕ X −

KEY: ☒ COMPLETED
⊟ UNCOMPLETED

DAILY CALLS

① X —	② X —	③ X —
④ X —	⑤ X —	⑥ X —
⑦ X —	⑧ X —	⑨ X —
⑩ X —	⑪ X —	⑫ X —
⑬ X —	⑭ X —	⑮ X —

"OOPS I FORGOT" - CARRY OVER TOMORROW

TO DO LIST #'S -

DAILY CALL #'S -

DAILY TASKS

DATE:

① X —
② X —
③ X —
④ X —
⑤ X —
⑥ X —
⑦ X —
⑧ X —
⑨ X —
⑩ X —
⑪ X —
⑫ X —
⑬ X —
⑭ X —
⑮ X —
⑯ X —
⑰ X —
⑱ X —
⑲ X —
⑳ X —
㉑ X —
㉒ X —
㉓ X —
㉔ X —
㉕ X —

KEY: ☒ COMPLETED
⊟ UNCOMPLETED

DAILY CALLS

① X ⊟	② X ⊟	③ X ⊟
④ X ⊟	⑤ X ⊟	⑥ X ⊟
⑦ X ⊟	⑧ X ⊟	⑨ X ⊟
⑩ X ⊟	⑪ X ⊟	⑫ X ⊟
⑬ X ⊟	⑭ X ⊟	⑮ X ⊟

"OOPS I FORGOT" - CARRY OVER TOMORROW

TO DO LIST #'S -

DAILY CALL #'S -

DAILY TASKS

DATE:

① X ⊟
② X ⊟
③ X ⊟
④ X ⊟
⑤ X ⊟
⑥ X ⊟
⑦ X ⊟
⑧ X ⊟
⑨ X ⊟
⑩ X ⊟
⑪ X ⊟
⑫ X ⊟
⑬ X ⊟
⑭ X ⊟
⑮ X ⊟
⑯ X ⊟
⑰ X ⊟
⑱ X ⊟
⑲ X ⊟
⑳ X ⊟
㉑ X ⊟
㉒ X ⊟
㉓ X ⊟
㉔ X ⊟
㉕ X ⊟

KEY: [X] COMPLETED
      [—] UNCOMPLETED

DAILY CALLS

(1) [X] [—]   (2) [X] [—]   (3) [X] [—]

(4) [X] [—]   (5) [X] [—]   (6) [X] [—]

(7) [X] [—]   (8) [X] [—]   (9) [X] [—]

(10) [X] [—]   (11) [X] [—]   (12) [X] [—]

(13) [X] [—]   (14) [X] [—]   (15) [X] [—]

"OOPS I FORGOT" - CARRY OVER TOMORROW

TO DO LIST #'S -

DAILY CALL #'S -

DAILY TASKS

DATE:

(1) X —
(2) X —
(3) X —
(4) X —
(5) X —
(6) X —
(7) X —
(8) X —
(9) X —
(10) X —
(11) X —
(12) X —
(13) X —
(14) X —
(15) X —
(16) X —
(17) X —
(18) X —
(19) X —
(20) X —
(21) X —
(22) X —
(23) X —
(24) X —
(25) X —

KEY: ☒ COMPLETED
⊟ UNCOMPLETED

DAILY CALLS

1 X —	2 X —	3 X —
4 X —	5 X —	6 X —
7 X —	8 X —	9 X —
10 X —	11 X —	12 X —
13 X —	14 X —	15 X —

"OOPS I FORGOT" - CARRY OVER TOMORROW

TO DO LIST #'S -

DAILY CALL #'S -

DAILY TASKS

DATE:

1. X —
2. X —
3. X —
4. X —
5. X —
6. X —
7. X —
8. X —
9. X —
10. X —
11. X —
12. X —
13. X —
14. X —
15. X —
16. X —
17. X —
18. X —
19. X —
20. X —
21. X —
22. X —
23. X —
24. X —
25. X —

KEY: ☒ COMPLETED
      ⊟ UNCOMPLETED

DAILY CALLS

① X —	② X —	③ X —
④ X —	⑤ X —	⑥ X —
⑦ X —	⑧ X —	⑨ X —
⑩ X —	⑪ X —	⑫ X —
⑬ X —	⑭ X —	⑮ X —

"OOPS I FORGOT" - CARRY OVER TOMORROW

TO DO LIST #'S -

DAILY CALL #'S -

DAILY TASKS

DATE:

① X —
② X —
③ X —
④ X —
⑤ X —
⑥ X —
⑦ X —
⑧ X —
⑨ X —
⑩ X —
⑪ X —
⑫ X —
⑬ X —
⑭ X —
⑮ X —
⑯ X —
⑰ X —
⑱ X —
⑲ X —
⑳ X —
㉑ X —
㉒ X —
㉓ X —
㉔ X —
㉕ X —

KEY: ☒ COMPLETED
      ⊟ UNCOMPLETED

DAILY CALLS

① X —   ② X —   ③ X —

④ X —   ⑤ X —   ⑥ X —

⑦ X —   ⑧ X —   ⑨ X —

⑩ X —   ⑪ X —   ⑫ X —

⑬ X —   ⑭ X —   ⑮ X —

"OOPS I FORGOT" - CARRY OVER TOMORROW

TO DO LIST #'S -

DAILY CALL #'S -

DAILY TASKS

DATE:

① X —
② X —
③ X —
④ X —
⑤ X —
⑥ X —
⑦ X —
⑧ X —
⑨ X —
⑩ X —
⑪ X —
⑫ X —
⑬ X —
⑭ X —
⑮ X —
⑯ X —
⑰ X —
⑱ X —
⑲ X —
⑳ X —
㉑ X —
㉒ X —
㉓ X —
㉔ X —
㉕ X —

KEY: ☒ COMPLETED
☐ UNCOMPLETED

DAILY CALLS

① X ☐	② X ☐	③ X ☐
④ X ☐	⑤ X ☐	⑥ X ☐
⑦ X ☐	⑧ X ☐	⑨ X ☐
⑩ X ☐	⑪ X ☐	⑫ X ☐
⑬ X ☐	⑭ X ☐	⑮ X ☐

"OOPS I FORGOT" - CARRY OVER TOMORROW

TO DO LIST #'S -

DAILY CALL #'S -

DAILY TASKS

DATE:

① X —
② X —
③ X —
④ X —
⑤ X —
⑥ X —
⑦ X —
⑧ X —
⑨ X —
⑩ X —
⑪ X —
⑫ X —
⑬ X —
⑭ X —
⑮ X —
⑯ X —
⑰ X —
⑱ X —
⑲ X —
⑳ X —
㉑ X —
㉒ X —
㉓ X —
㉔ X —
㉕ X —

KEY: ☒ COMPLETED
☐ UNCOMPLETED

DAILY CALLS

① X —   ② X —   ③ X —

④ X —   ⑤ X —   ⑥ X —

⑦ X —   ⑧ X —   ⑨ X —

⑩ X —   ⑪ X —   ⑫ X —

⑬ X —   ⑭ X —   ⑮ X —

"OOPS I FORGOT" - CARRY OVER TOMORROW

TO DO LIST #'S -

DAILY CALL #'S -

DAILY TASKS

DATE:

① X —
② X —
③ X —
④ X —
⑤ X —
⑥ X —
⑦ X —
⑧ X —
⑨ X —
⑩ X —
⑪ X —
⑫ X —
⑬ X —
⑭ X —
⑮ X —
⑯ X —
⑰ X —
⑱ X —
⑲ X —
⑳ X —
㉑ X —
㉒ X —
㉓ X —
㉔ X —
㉕ X —

KEY: ☒ COMPLETED
⊟ UNCOMPLETED

DAILY CALLS

① X — ② X — ③ X —

④ X — ⑤ X — ⑥ X —

⑦ X — ⑧ X — ⑨ X —

⑩ X — ⑪ X — ⑫ X —

⑬ X — ⑭ X — ⑮ X —

"OOPS I FORGOT" - CARRY OVER TOMORROW

TO DO LIST #'S -

DAILY CALL #'S -

DAILY TASKS

DATE:

① X —
② X —
③ X —
④ X —
⑤ X —
⑥ X —
⑦ X —
⑧ X —
⑨ X —
⑩ X —
⑪ X —
⑫ X —
⑬ X —
⑭ X —
⑮ X —
⑯ X —
⑰ X —
⑱ X —
⑲ X —
⑳ X —
㉑ X —
㉒ X —
㉓ X —
㉔ X —
㉕ X —

KEY: ☒ COMPLETED
⊟ UNCOMPLETED

DAILY CALLS

① X ⊟	② X ⊟	③ X ⊟
④ X ⊟	⑤ X ⊟	⑥ X ⊟
⑦ X ⊟	⑧ X ⊟	⑨ X ⊟
⑩ X ⊟	⑪ X ⊟	⑫ X ⊟
⑬ X ⊟	⑭ X ⊟	⑮ X ⊟

"OOPS I FORGOT" - CARRY OVER TOMORROW

TO DO LIST #'S -

DAILY CALL #'S -

DAILY TASKS

DATE:

① X ⊟
② X ⊟
③ X ⊟
④ X ⊟
⑤ X ⊟
⑥ X ⊟
⑦ X ⊟
⑧ X ⊟
⑨ X ⊟
⑩ X ⊟
⑪ X ⊟
⑫ X ⊟
⑬ X ⊟
⑭ X ⊟
⑮ X ⊟
⑯ X ⊟
⑰ X ⊟
⑱ X ⊟
⑲ X ⊟
⑳ X ⊟
㉑ X ⊟
㉒ X ⊟
㉓ X ⊟
㉔ X ⊟
㉕ X ⊟

KEY: ☒ COMPLETED ☐ UNCOMPLETED

DAILY CALLS

① X ☐	② X ☐	③ X ☐
④ X ☐	⑤ X ☐	⑥ X ☐
⑦ X ☐	⑧ X ☐	⑨ X ☐
⑩ X ☐	⑪ X ☐	⑫ X ☐
⑬ X ☐	⑭ X ☐	⑮ X ☐

"OOPS I FORGOT" - CARRY OVER TOMORROW

TO DO LIST #'S -

DAILY CALL #'S -

DAILY TASKS

DATE:

1. X ☐
2. X ☐
3. X ☐
4. X ☐
5. X ☐
6. X ☐
7. X ☐
8. X ☐
9. X ☐
10. X ☐
11. X ☐
12. X ☐
13. X ☐
14. X ☐
15. X ☐
16. X ☐
17. X ☐
18. X ☐
19. X ☐
20. X ☐
21. X ☐
22. X ☐
23. X ☐
24. X ☐
25. X ☐

KEY: ☒ COMPLETED
☐ UNCOMPLETED

DAILY CALLS

① X ☐	② X ☐	③ X ☐
④ X ☐	⑤ X ☐	⑥ X ☐
⑦ X ☐	⑧ X ☐	⑨ X ☐
⑩ X ☐	⑪ X ☐	⑫ X ☐
⑬ X ☐	⑭ X ☐	⑮ X ☐

"OOPS I FORGOT" - CARRY OVER TOMORROW

TO DO LIST #'S -

DAILY CALL #'S -

DAILY TASKS

DATE:

1. X ☐
2. X ☐
3. X ☐
4. X ☐
5. X ☐
6. X ☐
7. X ☐
8. X ☐
9. X ☐
10. X ☐
11. X ☐
12. X ☐
13. X ☐
14. X ☐
15. X ☐
16. X ☐
17. X ☐
18. X ☐
19. X ☐
20. X ☐
21. X ☐
22. X ☐
23. X ☐
24. X ☐
25. X ☐

KEY: ☒ COMPLETED
☐ UNCOMPLETED

DAILY CALLS

(1) X —	(2) X —	(3) X —
(4) X —	(5) X —	(6) X —
(7) X —	(8) X —	(9) X —
(10) X —	(11) X —	(12) X —
(13) X —	(14) X —	(15) X —

"OOPS I FORGOT" - CARRY OVER TOMORROW

TO DO LIST #'S -

DAILY CALL #'S -

DAILY TASKS

DATE:

(1) X —
(2) X —
(3) X —
(4) X —
(5) X —
(6) X —
(7) X —
(8) X —
(9) X —
(10) X —
(11) X —
(12) X —
(13) X —
(14) X —
(15) X —
(16) X —
(17) X —
(18) X —
(19) X —
(20) X —
(21) X —
(22) X —
(23) X —
(24) X —
(25) X —

KEY: X COMPLETED
      — UNCOMPLETED

DAILY CALLS

① X —   ② X —   ③ X —

④ X —   ⑤ X —   ⑥ X —

⑦ X —   ⑧ X —   ⑨ X —

⑩ X —   ⑪ X —   ⑫ X —

⑬ X —   ⑭ X —   ⑮ X —

"OOPS I FORGOT" - CARRY OVER TOMORROW

TO DO LIST #'S -

DAILY CALL #'S -

DAILY TASKS

DATE:

① X —
② X —
③ X —
④ X —
⑤ X —
⑥ X —
⑦ X —
⑧ X —
⑨ X —
⑩ X —
⑪ X —
⑫ X —
⑬ X —
⑭ X —
⑮ X —
⑯ X —
⑰ X —
⑱ X —
⑲ X —
⑳ X —
㉑ X —
㉒ X —
㉓ X —
㉔ X —
㉕ X —

KEY: ☒ COMPLETED
☐− UNCOMPLETED

DAILY CALLS

① X −
② X −
③ X −
④ X −
⑤ X −
⑥ X −
⑦ X −
⑧ X −
⑨ X −
⑩ X −
⑪ X −
⑫ X −
⑬ X −
⑭ X −
⑮ X −

"OOPS I FORGOT" - CARRY OVER TOMORROW

TO DO LIST #'S -

DAILY CALL #'S -

DAILY TASKS

DATE:

① X −
② X −
③ X −
④ X −
⑤ X −
⑥ X −
⑦ X −
⑧ X −
⑨ X −
⑩ X −
⑪ X −
⑫ X −
⑬ X −
⑭ X −
⑮ X −
⑯ X −
⑰ X −
⑱ X −
⑲ X −
⑳ X −
㉑ X −
㉒ X −
㉓ X −
㉔ X −
㉕ X −

KEY: ☒ COMPLETED
      ⊟ UNCOMPLETED

DAILY CALLS

① X —	② X —	③ X —
④ X —	⑤ X —	⑥ X —
⑦ X —	⑧ X —	⑨ X —
⑩ X —	⑪ X —	⑫ X —
⑬ X —	⑭ X —	⑮ X —

"OOPS I FORGOT" - CARRY OVER TOMORROW

TO DO LIST #'S -

DAILY CALL #'S -

DAILY TASKS

DATE:

① X —
② X —
③ X —
④ X —
⑤ X —
⑥ X —
⑦ X —
⑧ X —
⑨ X —
⑩ X —
⑪ X —
⑫ X —
⑬ X —
⑭ X —
⑮ X —
⑯ X —
⑰ X —
⑱ X —
⑲ X —
⑳ X —
㉑ X —
㉒ X —
㉓ X —
㉔ X —
㉕ X —

KEY: ☒ COMPLETED ⊟ UNCOMPLETED

DAILY CALLS

① X —
② X —
③ X —
④ X —
⑤ X —
⑥ X —
⑦ X —
⑧ X —
⑨ X —
⑩ X —
⑪ X —
⑫ X —
⑬ X —
⑭ X —
⑮ X —

"OOPS I FORGOT" - CARRY OVER TOMORROW

TO DO LIST #'S -

DAILY CALL #'S -

DAILY TASKS

DATE:

① X —
② X —
③ X —
④ X —
⑤ X —
⑥ X —
⑦ X —
⑧ X —
⑨ X —
⑩ X —
⑪ X —
⑫ X —
⑬ X —
⑭ X —
⑮ X —
⑯ X —
⑰ X —
⑱ X —
⑲ X —
⑳ X —
㉑ X —
㉒ X —
㉓ X —
㉔ X —
㉕ X —

KEY: ☒ COMPLETED
☐ UNCOMPLETED

DAILY CALLS

① X ─	② X ─	③ X ─
④ X ─	⑤ X ─	⑥ X ─
⑦ X ─	⑧ X ─	⑨ X ─
⑩ X ─	⑪ X ─	⑫ X ─
⑬ X ─	⑭ X ─	⑮ X ─

"OOPS I FORGOT" - CARRY OVER TOMORROW

TO DO LIST #'S -

DAILY CALL #'S -

DAILY TASKS

DATE:

① X ─
② X ─
③ X ─
④ X ─
⑤ X ─
⑥ X ─
⑦ X ─
⑧ X ─
⑨ X ─
⑩ X ─
⑪ X ─
⑫ X ─
⑬ X ─
⑭ X ─
⑮ X ─
⑯ X ─
⑰ X ─
⑱ X ─
⑲ X ─
⑳ X ─
㉑ X ─
㉒ X ─
㉓ X ─
㉔ X ─
㉕ X ─

KEY: [X] COMPLETED [—] UNCOMPLETED

DAILY CALLS

(1) [X] [—]　(2) [X] [—]　(3) [X] [—]

(4) [X] [—]　(5) [X] [—]　(6) [X] [—]

(7) [X] [—]　(8) [X] [—]　(9) [X] [—]

(10) [X] [—]　(11) [X] [—]　(12) [X] [—]

(13) [X] [—]　(14) [X] [—]　(15) [X] [—]

"OOPS I FORGOT" - CARRY OVER TOMORROW

TO DO LIST #'S -

DAILY CALL #'S -

DAILY TASKS

DATE:

(1) [X] [—]
(2) [X] [—]
(3) [X] [—]
(4) [X] [—]
(5) [X] [—]
(6) [X] [—]
(7) [X] [—]
(8) [X] [—]
(9) [X] [—]
(10) [X] [—]
(11) [X] [—]
(12) [X] [—]
(13) [X] [—]
(14) [X] [—]
(15) [X] [—]
(16) [X] [—]
(17) [X] [—]
(18) [X] [—]
(19) [X] [—]
(20) [X] [—]
(21) [X] [—]
(22) [X] [—]
(23) [X] [—]
(24) [X] [—]
(25) [X] [—]

KEY: ☒ COMPLETED
⊟ UNCOMPLETED

DAILY CALLS

① ☒ ⊟
② ☒ ⊟
③ ☒ ⊟
④ ☒ ⊟
⑤ ☒ ⊟
⑥ ☒ ⊟
⑦ ☒ ⊟
⑧ ☒ ⊟
⑨ ☒ ⊟
⑩ ☒ ⊟
⑪ ☒ ⊟
⑫ ☒ ⊟
⑬ ☒ ⊟
⑭ ☒ ⊟
⑮ ☒ ⊟

"OOPS I FORGOT" - CARRY OVER TOMORROW

TO DO LIST #'S -

DAILY CALL #'S -

DAILY TASKS

DATE:

① ☒ ⊟
② ☒ ⊟
③ ☒ ⊟
④ ☒ ⊟
⑤ ☒ ⊟
⑥ ☒ ⊟
⑦ ☒ ⊟
⑧ ☒ ⊟
⑨ ☒ ⊟
⑩ ☒ ⊟
⑪ ☒ ⊟
⑫ ☒ ⊟
⑬ ☒ ⊟
⑭ ☒ ⊟
⑮ ☒ ⊟
⑯ ☒ ⊟
⑰ ☒ ⊟
⑱ ☒ ⊟
⑲ ☒ ⊟
⑳ ☒ ⊟
㉑ ☒ ⊟
㉒ ☒ ⊟
㉓ ☒ ⊟
㉔ ☒ ⊟
㉕ ☒ ⊟

KEY: ☒ COMPLETED
⊟ UNCOMPLETED

DAILY CALLS

① ☒ ⊟   ② ☒ ⊟   ③ ☒ ⊟

④ ☒ ⊟   ⑤ ☒ ⊟   ⑥ ☒ ⊟

⑦ ☒ ⊟   ⑧ ☒ ⊟   ⑨ ☒ ⊟

⑩ ☒ ⊟   ⑪ ☒ ⊟   ⑫ ☒ ⊟

⑬ ☒ ⊟   ⑭ ☒ ⊟   ⑮ ☒ ⊟

"OOPS I FORGOT" - CARRY OVER TOMORROW

TO DO LIST #'S -

DAILY CALL #'S -

DAILY TASKS

DATE:

① ☒ ⊟
② ☒ ⊟
③ ☒ ⊟
④ ☒ ⊟
⑤ ☒ ⊟
⑥ ☒ ⊟
⑦ ☒ ⊟
⑧ ☒ ⊟
⑨ ☒ ⊟
⑩ ☒ ⊟
⑪ ☒ ⊟
⑫ ☒ ⊟
⑬ ☒ ⊟
⑭ ☒ ⊟
⑮ ☒ ⊟
⑯ ☒ ⊟
⑰ ☒ ⊟
⑱ ☒ ⊟
⑲ ☒ ⊟
⑳ ☒ ⊟
㉑ ☒ ⊟
㉒ ☒ ⊟
㉓ ☒ ⊟
㉔ ☒ ⊟
㉕ ☒ ⊟

KEY: ☒ COMPLETED
☐ UNCOMPLETED

DAILY CALLS

① X ☐	② X ☐	③ X ☐
④ X ☐	⑤ X ☐	⑥ X ☐
⑦ X ☐	⑧ X ☐	⑨ X ☐
⑩ X ☐	⑪ X ☐	⑫ X ☐
⑬ X ☐	⑭ X ☐	⑮ X ☐

"OOPS I FORGOT" - CARRY OVER TOMORROW

TO DO LIST #'S -

DAILY CALL #'S -

DAILY TASKS

DATE:

① X ☐
② X ☐
③ X ☐
④ X ☐
⑤ X ☐
⑥ X ☐
⑦ X ☐
⑧ X ☐
⑨ X ☐
⑩ X ☐
⑪ X ☐
⑫ X ☐
⑬ X ☐
⑭ X ☐
⑮ X ☐
⑯ X ☐
⑰ X ☐
⑱ X ☐
⑲ X ☐
⑳ X ☐
㉑ X ☐
㉒ X ☐
㉓ X ☐
㉔ X ☐
㉕ X ☐

KEY: ☒ COMPLETED
☐— UNCOMPLETED

DAILY CALLS

① X —	② X —	③ X —
④ X —	⑤ X —	⑥ X —
⑦ X —	⑧ X —	⑨ X —
⑩ X —	⑪ X —	⑫ X —
⑬ X —	⑭ X —	⑮ X —

"OOPS I FORGOT" - CARRY OVER TOMORROW

TO DO LIST #'S -

DAILY CALL #'S -

DAILY TASKS

DATE:

① X —
② X —
③ X —
④ X —
⑤ X —
⑥ X —
⑦ X —
⑧ X —
⑨ X —
⑩ X —
⑪ X —
⑫ X —
⑬ X —
⑭ X —
⑮ X —
⑯ X —
⑰ X —
⑱ X —
⑲ X —
⑳ X —
㉑ X —
㉒ X —
㉓ X —
㉔ X —
㉕ X —

KEY: [X] COMPLETED
      [—] UNCOMPLETED

DAILY CALLS

① [X][—]	② [X][—]	③ [X][—]
④ [X][—]	⑤ [X][—]	⑥ [X][—]
⑦ [X][—]	⑧ [X][—]	⑨ [X][—]
⑩ [X][—]	⑪ [X][—]	⑫ [X][—]
⑬ [X][—]	⑭ [X][—]	⑮ [X][—]

"OOPS I FORGOT" - CARRY OVER TOMORROW

TO DO LIST #'S -

DAILY CALL #'S -

DAILY TASKS

DATE:

① X —
② X —
③ X —
④ X —
⑤ X —
⑥ X —
⑦ X —
⑧ X —
⑨ X —
⑩ X —
⑪ X —
⑫ X —
⑬ X —
⑭ X —
⑮ X —
⑯ X —
⑰ X —
⑱ X —
⑲ X —
⑳ X —
㉑ X —
㉒ X —
㉓ X —
㉔ X —
㉕ X —

KEY: ☒ COMPLETED
☐ UNCOMPLETED

DAILY CALLS

① X —	② X —	③ X —
④ X —	⑤ X —	⑥ X —
⑦ X —	⑧ X —	⑨ X —
⑩ X —	⑪ X —	⑫ X —
⑬ X —	⑭ X —	⑮ X —

"OOPS I FORGOT" - CARRY OVER TOMORROW

TO DO LIST #'S -

DAILY CALL #'S -

DAILY TASKS

DATE:

① X —
② X —
③ X —
④ X —
⑤ X —
⑥ X —
⑦ X —
⑧ X —
⑨ X —
⑩ X —
⑪ X —
⑫ X —
⑬ X —
⑭ X —
⑮ X —
⑯ X —
⑰ X —
⑱ X —
⑲ X —
⑳ X —
㉑ X —
㉒ X —
㉓ X —
㉔ X —
㉕ X —

KEY: ☒ COMPLETED
☐ UNCOMPLETED

DAILY CALLS

① X ─
② X ─
③ X ─
④ X ─
⑤ X ─
⑥ X ─
⑦ X ─
⑧ X ─
⑨ X ─
⑩ X ─
⑪ X ─
⑫ X ─
⑬ X ─
⑭ X ─
⑮ X ─

"OOPS I FORGOT" - CARRY OVER TOMORROW

TO DO LIST #'S -

DAILY CALL #'S -

DAILY TASKS
DATE:

① X ─
② X ─
③ X ─
④ X ─
⑤ X ─
⑥ X ─
⑦ X ─
⑧ X ─
⑨ X ─
⑩ X ─
⑪ X ─
⑫ X ─
⑬ X ─
⑭ X ─
⑮ X ─
⑯ X ─
⑰ X ─
⑱ X ─
⑲ X ─
⑳ X ─
㉑ X ─
㉒ X ─
㉓ X ─
㉔ X ─
㉕ X ─

KEY: ☒ COMPLETED
⊟ UNCOMPLETED

DAILY CALLS

① X ⊟	② X ⊟	③ X ⊟
④ X ⊟	⑤ X ⊟	⑥ X ⊟
⑦ X ⊟	⑧ X ⊟	⑨ X ⊟
⑩ X ⊟	⑪ X ⊟	⑫ X ⊟
⑬ X ⊟	⑭ X ⊟	⑮ X ⊟

"OOPS I FORGOT" - CARRY OVER TOMORROW

TO DO LIST #'S -

DAILY CALL #'S -

DAILY TASKS

DATE:

① X ⊟
② X ⊟
③ X ⊟
④ X ⊟
⑤ X ⊟
⑥ X ⊟
⑦ X ⊟
⑧ X ⊟
⑨ X ⊟
⑩ X ⊟
⑪ X ⊟
⑫ X ⊟
⑬ X ⊟
⑭ X ⊟
⑮ X ⊟
⑯ X ⊟
⑰ X ⊟
⑱ X ⊟
⑲ X ⊟
⑳ X ⊟
㉑ X ⊟
㉒ X ⊟
㉓ X ⊟
㉔ X ⊟
㉕ X ⊟

KEY: ☒ COMPLETED
☐ UNCOMPLETED

DAILY CALLS

① ☒ ☐ ② ☒ ☐ ③ ☒ ☐

④ ☒ ☐ ⑤ ☒ ☐ ⑥ ☒ ☐

⑦ ☒ ☐ ⑧ ☒ ☐ ⑨ ☒ ☐

⑩ ☒ ☐ ⑪ ☒ ☐ ⑫ ☒ ☐

⑬ ☒ ☐ ⑭ ☒ ☐ ⑮ ☒ ☐

"OOPS I FORGOT" - CARRY OVER TOMORROW

TO DO LIST #'S -

DAILY CALL #'S -

DAILY TASKS

DATE:

① ☒ ☐
② ☒ ☐
③ ☒ ☐
④ ☒ ☐
⑤ ☒ ☐
⑥ ☒ ☐
⑦ ☒ ☐
⑧ ☒ ☐
⑨ ☒ ☐
⑩ ☒ ☐
⑪ ☒ ☐
⑫ ☒ ☐
⑬ ☒ ☐
⑭ ☒ ☐
⑮ ☒ ☐
⑯ ☒ ☐
⑰ ☒ ☐
⑱ ☒ ☐
⑲ ☒ ☐
⑳ ☒ ☐
㉑ ☒ ☐
㉒ ☒ ☐
㉓ ☒ ☐
㉔ ☒ ☐
㉕ ☒ ☐

KEY: ☒ COMPLETED
☐— UNCOMPLETED

DAILY CALLS

① X —	② X —	③ X —
④ X —	⑤ X —	⑥ X —
⑦ X —	⑧ X —	⑨ X —
⑩ X —	⑪ X —	⑫ X —
⑬ X —	⑭ X —	⑮ X —

"OOPS I FORGOT" - CARRY OVER TOMORROW

TO DO LIST #'S -

DAILY CALL #'S -

DAILY TASKS

DATE:

① X —
② X —
③ X —
④ X —
⑤ X —
⑥ X —
⑦ X —
⑧ X —
⑨ X —
⑩ X —
⑪ X —
⑫ X —
⑬ X —
⑭ X —
⑮ X —
⑯ X —
⑰ X —
⑱ X —
⑲ X —
⑳ X —
㉑ X —
㉒ X —
㉓ X —
㉔ X —
㉕ X —

KEY: ☒ COMPLETED
☐ UNCOMPLETED

DAILY CALLS

① ☒ ☐
② ☒ ☐
③ ☒ ☐
④ ☒ ☐
⑤ ☒ ☐
⑥ ☒ ☐
⑦ ☒ ☐
⑧ ☒ ☐
⑨ ☒ ☐
⑩ ☒ ☐
⑪ ☒ ☐
⑫ ☒ ☐
⑬ ☒ ☐
⑭ ☒ ☐
⑮ ☒ ☐

"OOPS I FORGOT" - CARRY OVER TOMORROW

TO DO LIST #'S -

DAILY CALL #'S -

DAILY TASKS

DATE:

① ☒ ☐
② ☒ ☐
③ ☒ ☐
④ ☒ ☐
⑤ ☒ ☐
⑥ ☒ ☐
⑦ ☒ ☐
⑧ ☒ ☐
⑨ ☒ ☐
⑩ ☒ ☐
⑪ ☒ ☐
⑫ ☒ ☐
⑬ ☒ ☐
⑭ ☒ ☐
⑮ ☒ ☐
⑯ ☒ ☐
⑰ ☒ ☐
⑱ ☒ ☐
⑲ ☒ ☐
⑳ ☒ ☐
㉑ ☒ ☐
㉒ ☒ ☐
㉓ ☒ ☐
㉔ ☒ ☐
㉕ ☒ ☐

KEY: ☒ COMPLETED
⊟ UNCOMPLETED

DAILY CALLS

① X ⊟   ② X ⊟   ③ X ⊟

④ X ⊟   ⑤ X ⊟   ⑥ X ⊟

⑦ X ⊟   ⑧ X ⊟   ⑨ X ⊟

⑩ X ⊟   ⑪ X ⊟   ⑫ X ⊟

⑬ X ⊟   ⑭ X ⊟   ⑮ X ⊟

"OOPS I FORGOT" - CARRY OVER TOMORROW

TO DO LIST #'S -

DAILY CALL #'S -

DAILY TASKS

DATE:

① X ⊟
② X ⊟
③ X ⊟
④ X ⊟
⑤ X ⊟
⑥ X ⊟
⑦ X ⊟
⑧ X ⊟
⑨ X ⊟
⑩ X ⊟
⑪ X ⊟
⑫ X ⊟
⑬ X ⊟
⑭ X ⊟
⑮ X ⊟
⑯ X ⊟
⑰ X ⊟
⑱ X ⊟
⑲ X ⊟
⑳ X ⊟
㉑ X ⊟
㉒ X ⊟
㉓ X ⊟
㉔ X ⊟
㉕ X ⊟

KEY: ☒ COMPLETED
      ⊟ UNCOMPLETED

DAILY CALLS

① X —   ② X —   ③ X —

④ X —   ⑤ X —   ⑥ X —

⑦ X —   ⑧ X —   ⑨ X —

⑩ X —   ⑪ X —   ⑫ X —

⑬ X —   ⑭ X —   ⑮ X —

"OOPS I FORGOT" - CARRY OVER TOMORROW

TO DO LIST #'S -

DAILY CALL #'S -

DAILY TASKS

DATE:

① X —
② X —
③ X —
④ X —
⑤ X —
⑥ X —
⑦ X —
⑧ X —
⑨ X —
⑩ X —
⑪ X —
⑫ X —
⑬ X —
⑭ X —
⑮ X —
⑯ X —
⑰ X —
⑱ X —
⑲ X —
⑳ X —
㉑ X —
㉒ X —
㉓ X —
㉔ X —
㉕ X —

KEY: ☒ COMPLETED
⊟ UNCOMPLETED

DAILY CALLS

(1) X —
(2) X —
(3) X —
(4) X —
(5) X —
(6) X —
(7) X —
(8) X —
(9) X —
(10) X —
(11) X —
(12) X —
(13) X —
(14) X —
(15) X —

"OOPS I FORGOT" - CARRY OVER TOMORROW

TO DO LIST #'S -

DAILY CALL #'S -

DAILY TASKS

DATE:

(1) X —
(2) X —
(3) X —
(4) X —
(5) X —
(6) X —
(7) X —
(8) X —
(9) X —
(10) X —
(11) X —
(12) X —
(13) X —
(14) X —
(15) X —
(16) X —
(17) X —
(18) X —
(19) X —
(20) X —
(21) X —
(22) X —
(23) X —
(24) X —
(25) X —

KEY: ☒ COMPLETED
☐— UNCOMPLETED

DAILY CALLS

① X —	② X —	③ X —
④ X —	⑤ X —	⑥ X —
⑦ X —	⑧ X —	⑨ X —
⑩ X —	⑪ X —	⑫ X —
⑬ X —	⑭ X —	⑮ X —

"OOPS I FORGOT" - CARRY OVER TOMORROW

TO DO LIST #'S -

DAILY CALL #'S -

DAILY TASKS

DATE:

① X —
② X —
③ X —
④ X —
⑤ X —
⑥ X —
⑦ X —
⑧ X —
⑨ X —
⑩ X —
⑪ X —
⑫ X —
⑬ X —
⑭ X —
⑮ X —
⑯ X —
⑰ X —
⑱ X —
⑲ X —
⑳ X —
㉑ X —
㉒ X —
㉓ X —
㉔ X —
㉕ X —

KEY: ☒ COMPLETED   ⊟ UNCOMPLETED

DAILY CALLS

① X —	② X —	③ X —
④ X —	⑤ X —	⑥ X —
⑦ X —	⑧ X —	⑨ X —
⑩ X —	⑪ X —	⑫ X —
⑬ X —	⑭ X —	⑮ X —

"OOPS I FORGOT" - CARRY OVER TOMORROW

TO DO LIST #'S -

DAILY CALL #'S -

DAILY TASKS

DATE:

① X —
② X —
③ X —
④ X —
⑤ X —
⑥ X —
⑦ X —
⑧ X —
⑨ X —
⑩ X —
⑪ X —
⑫ X —
⑬ X —
⑭ X —
⑮ X —
⑯ X —
⑰ X —
⑱ X —
⑲ X —
⑳ X —
㉑ X —
㉒ X —
㉓ X —
㉔ X —
㉕ X —

KEY: [X] COMPLETED
      [—] UNCOMPLETED

DAILY CALLS

① [X][—]　② [X][—]　③ [X][—]

④ [X][—]　⑤ [X][—]　⑥ [X][—]

⑦ [X][—]　⑧ [X][—]　⑨ [X][—]

⑩ [X][—]　⑪ [X][—]　⑫ [X][—]

⑬ [X][—]　⑭ [X][—]　⑮ [X][—]

"OOPS I FORGOT" - CARRY OVER TOMORROW

TO DO LIST #'S -

DAILY CALL #'S -

DAILY TASKS

DATE:

① [X][—]
② [X][—]
③ [X][—]
④ [X][—]
⑤ [X][—]
⑥ [X][—]
⑦ [X][—]
⑧ [X][—]
⑨ [X][—]
⑩ [X][—]
⑪ [X][—]
⑫ [X][—]
⑬ [X][—]
⑭ [X][—]
⑮ [X][—]
⑯ [X][—]
⑰ [X][—]
⑱ [X][—]
⑲ [X][—]
⑳ [X][—]
㉑ [X][—]
㉒ [X][—]
㉓ [X][—]
㉔ [X][—]
㉕ [X][—]

KEY: ☒ COMPLETED
☐— UNCOMPLETED

DAILY CALLS

① ☒ ☐—	② ☒ ☐—	③ ☒ ☐—
④ ☒ ☐—	⑤ ☒ ☐—	⑥ ☒ ☐—
⑦ ☒ ☐—	⑧ ☒ ☐—	⑨ ☒ ☐—
⑩ ☒ ☐—	⑪ ☒ ☐—	⑫ ☒ ☐—
⑬ ☒ ☐—	⑭ ☒ ☐—	⑮ ☒ ☐—

"OOPS I FORGOT" - CARRY OVER TOMORROW

TO DO LIST #'S -

DAILY CALL #'S -

DAILY TASKS

DATE:

① X —
② X —
③ X —
④ X —
⑤ X —
⑥ X —
⑦ X —
⑧ X —
⑨ X —
⑩ X —
⑪ X —
⑫ X —
⑬ X —
⑭ X —
⑮ X —
⑯ X —
⑰ X —
⑱ X —
⑲ X —
⑳ X —
㉑ X —
㉒ X —
㉓ X —
㉔ X —
㉕ X —

KEY: ☒ COMPLETED
☐— UNCOMPLETED

DAILY CALLS

① X —	② X —	③ X —
④ X —	⑤ X —	⑥ X —
⑦ X —	⑧ X —	⑨ X —
⑩ X —	⑪ X —	⑫ X —
⑬ X —	⑭ X —	⑮ X —

"OOPS I FORGOT" - CARRY OVER TOMORROW

TO DO LIST #'S -

DAILY CALL #'S -

DAILY TASKS
DATE:

① X —
② X —
③ X —
④ X —
⑤ X —
⑥ X —
⑦ X —
⑧ X —
⑨ X —
⑩ X —
⑪ X —
⑫ X —
⑬ X —
⑭ X —
⑮ X —
⑯ X —
⑰ X —
⑱ X —
⑲ X —
⑳ X —
㉑ X —
㉒ X —
㉓ X —
㉔ X —
㉕ X —

KEY: ☒ COMPLETED ⊟ UNCOMPLETED

DAILY CALLS

① X —	② X —	③ X —
④ X —	⑤ X —	⑥ X —
⑦ X —	⑧ X —	⑨ X —
⑩ X —	⑪ X —	⑫ X —
⑬ X —	⑭ X —	⑮ X —

"OOPS I FORGOT" - CARRY OVER TOMORROW

TO DO LIST #'S -

DAILY CALL #'S -

DAILY TASKS

DATE:

① X —
② X —
③ X —
④ X —
⑤ X —
⑥ X —
⑦ X —
⑧ X —
⑨ X —
⑩ X —
⑪ X —
⑫ X —
⑬ X —
⑭ X —
⑮ X —
⑯ X —
⑰ X —
⑱ X —
⑲ X —
⑳ X —
㉑ X —
㉒ X —
㉓ X —
㉔ X —
㉕ X —

KEY: ☒ COMPLETED
⊟ UNCOMPLETED

DAILY CALLS

① X —   ② X —   ③ X —

④ X —   ⑤ X —   ⑥ X —

⑦ X —   ⑧ X —   ⑨ X —

⑩ X —   ⑪ X —   ⑫ X —

⑬ X —   ⑭ X —   ⑮ X —

"OOPS I FORGOT" - CARRY OVER TOMORROW

TO DO LIST #'S -

DAILY CALL #'S -

DAILY TASKS

DATE:

① X —
② X —
③ X —
④ X —
⑤ X —
⑥ X —
⑦ X —
⑧ X —
⑨ X —
⑩ X —
⑪ X —
⑫ X —
⑬ X —
⑭ X —
⑮ X —
⑯ X —
⑰ X —
⑱ X —
⑲ X —
⑳ X —
㉑ X —
㉒ X —
㉓ X —
㉔ X —
㉕ X —

KEY: ☒ COMPLETED
⊟ UNCOMPLETED

DAILY CALLS

1 ☒ ⊟	2 ☒ ⊟	3 ☒ ⊟
4 ☒ ⊟	5 ☒ ⊟	6 ☒ ⊟
7 ☒ ⊟	8 ☒ ⊟	9 ☒ ⊟
10 ☒ ⊟	11 ☒ ⊟	12 ☒ ⊟
13 ☒ ⊟	14 ☒ ⊟	15 ☒ ⊟

"OOPS I FORGOT" - CARRY OVER TOMORROW

TO DO LIST #'S -

DAILY CALL #'S -

DAILY TASKS

DATE:

1. ☒ ⊟
2. ☒ ⊟
3. ☒ ⊟
4. ☒ ⊟
5. ☒ ⊟
6. ☒ ⊟
7. ☒ ⊟
8. ☒ ⊟
9. ☒ ⊟
10. ☒ ⊟
11. ☒ ⊟
12. ☒ ⊟
13. ☒ ⊟
14. ☒ ⊟
15. ☒ ⊟
16. ☒ ⊟
17. ☒ ⊟
18. ☒ ⊟
19. ☒ ⊟
20. ☒ ⊟
21. ☒ ⊟
22. ☒ ⊟
23. ☒ ⊟
24. ☒ ⊟
25. ☒ ⊟

KEY: X COMPLETED
— UNCOMPLETED

DAILY CALLS

1 X —	2 X —	3 X —
4 X —	5 X —	6 X —
7 X —	8 X —	9 X —
10 X —	11 X —	12 X —
13 X —	14 X —	15 X —

"OOPS I FORGOT" - CARRY OVER TOMORROW

TO DO LIST #'S -

DAILY CALL #'S -

DAILY TASKS

DATE:

1. X —
2. X —
3. X —
4. X —
5. X —
6. X —
7. X —
8. X —
9. X —
10. X —
11. X —
12. X —
13. X —
14. X —
15. X —
16. X —
17. X —
18. X —
19. X —
20. X —
21. X —
22. X —
23. X —
24. X —
25. X —

KEY: [X] COMPLETED
[—] UNCOMPLETED

DAILY CALLS

(1) X —	(2) X —	(3) X —
(4) X —	(5) X —	(6) X —
(7) X —	(8) X —	(9) X —
(10) X —	(11) X —	(12) X —
(13) X —	(14) X —	(15) X —

"OOPS I FORGOT" - CARRY OVER TOMORROW

TO DO LIST #'S -

DAILY CALL #'S -

DAILY TASKS

DATE:

(1) X —
(2) X —
(3) X —
(4) X —
(5) X —
(6) X —
(7) X —
(8) X —
(9) X —
(10) X —
(11) X —
(12) X —
(13) X —
(14) X —
(15) X —
(16) X —
(17) X —
(18) X —
(19) X —
(20) X —
(21) X —
(22) X —
(23) X —
(24) X —
(25) X —

KEY: ☒ COMPLETED
☐— UNCOMPLETED

DAILY CALLS

① X —
② X —
③ X —
④ X —
⑤ X —
⑥ X —
⑦ X —
⑧ X —
⑨ X —
⑩ X —
⑪ X —
⑫ X —
⑬ X —
⑭ X —
⑮ X —

"OOPS I FORGOT" - CARRY OVER TOMORROW

TO DO LIST #'S -

DAILY CALL #'S -

DAILY TASKS

DATE:

① X —
② X —
③ X —
④ X —
⑤ X —
⑥ X —
⑦ X —
⑧ X —
⑨ X —
⑩ X —
⑪ X —
⑫ X —
⑬ X —
⑭ X —
⑮ X —
⑯ X —
⑰ X —
⑱ X —
⑲ X —
⑳ X —
㉑ X —
㉒ X —
㉓ X —
㉔ X —
㉕ X —

KEY: ☒ COMPLETED
⊟ UNCOMPLETED

DAILY CALLS

① ☒ ⊟   ② ☒ ⊟   ③ ☒ ⊟

④ ☒ ⊟   ⑤ ☒ ⊟   ⑥ ☒ ⊟

⑦ ☒ ⊟   ⑧ ☒ ⊟   ⑨ ☒ ⊟

⑩ ☒ ⊟   ⑪ ☒ ⊟   ⑫ ☒ ⊟

⑬ ☒ ⊟   ⑭ ☒ ⊟   ⑮ ☒ ⊟

"OOPS I FORGOT" - CARRY OVER TOMORROW

TO DO LIST #'S -

DAILY CALL #'S -

DAILY TASKS

DATE:

① ☒ ⊟
② ☒ ⊟
③ ☒ ⊟
④ ☒ ⊟
⑤ ☒ ⊟
⑥ ☒ ⊟
⑦ ☒ ⊟
⑧ ☒ ⊟
⑨ ☒ ⊟
⑩ ☒ ⊟
⑪ ☒ ⊟
⑫ ☒ ⊟
⑬ ☒ ⊟
⑭ ☒ ⊟
⑮ ☒ ⊟
⑯ ☒ ⊟
⑰ ☒ ⊟
⑱ ☒ ⊟
⑲ ☒ ⊟
⑳ ☒ ⊟
㉑ ☒ ⊟
㉒ ☒ ⊟
㉓ ☒ ⊟
㉔ ☒ ⊟
㉕ ☒ ⊟

KEY: [X] COMPLETED
[—] UNCOMPLETED

DAILY CALLS

(1) [X][—]	(2) [X][—]	(3) [X][—]
(4) [X][—]	(5) [X][—]	(6) [X][—]
(7) [X][—]	(8) [X][—]	(9) [X][—]
(10) [X][—]	(11) [X][—]	(12) [X][—]
(13) [X][—]	(14) [X][—]	(15) [X][—]

"OOPS I FORGOT" - CARRY OVER TOMORROW

TO DO LIST #'S -

DAILY CALL #'S -

DAILY TASKS

DATE:

(1) X —
(2) X —
(3) X —
(4) X —
(5) X —
(6) X —
(7) X —
(8) X —
(9) X —
(10) X —
(11) X —
(12) X —
(13) X —
(14) X —
(15) X —
(16) X —
(17) X —
(18) X —
(19) X —
(20) X —
(21) X —
(22) X —
(23) X —
(24) X —
(25) X —

KEY: ☒ COMPLETED
☐ UNCOMPLETED

DAILY CALLS

① X ☐	② X ☐	③ X ☐
④ X ☐	⑤ X ☐	⑥ X ☐
⑦ X ☐	⑧ X ☐	⑨ X ☐
⑩ X ☐	⑪ X ☐	⑫ X ☐
⑬ X ☐	⑭ X ☐	⑮ X ☐

"OOPS I FORGOT" - CARRY OVER TOMORROW

TO DO LIST #'S -

DAILY CALL #'S -

DAILY TASKS

DATE:

① X ☐
② X ☐
③ X ☐
④ X ☐
⑤ X ☐
⑥ X ☐
⑦ X ☐
⑧ X ☐
⑨ X ☐
⑩ X ☐
⑪ X ☐
⑫ X ☐
⑬ X ☐
⑭ X ☐
⑮ X ☐
⑯ X ☐
⑰ X ☐
⑱ X ☐
⑲ X ☐
⑳ X ☐
㉑ X ☐
㉒ X ☐
㉓ X ☐
㉔ X ☐
㉕ X ☐

KEY: ☒ COMPLETED
⊟ UNCOMPLETED

DAILY CALLS

① X ⊟   ② X ⊟   ③ X ⊟

④ X ⊟   ⑤ X ⊟   ⑥ X ⊟

⑦ X ⊟   ⑧ X ⊟   ⑨ X ⊟

⑩ X ⊟   ⑪ X ⊟   ⑫ X ⊟

⑬ X ⊟   ⑭ X ⊟   ⑮ X ⊟

"OOPS I FORGOT" - CARRY OVER TOMORROW

TO DO LIST #'S -

DAILY CALL #'S -

DAILY TASKS

DATE:

① X ⊟
② X ⊟
③ X ⊟
④ X ⊟
⑤ X ⊟
⑥ X ⊟
⑦ X ⊟
⑧ X ⊟
⑨ X ⊟
⑩ X ⊟
⑪ X ⊟
⑫ X ⊟
⑬ X ⊟
⑭ X ⊟
⑮ X ⊟
⑯ X ⊟
⑰ X ⊟
⑱ X ⊟
⑲ X ⊟
⑳ X ⊟
㉑ X ⊟
㉒ X ⊟
㉓ X ⊟
㉔ X ⊟
㉕ X ⊟

KEY: ☒ COMPLETED ⊟ UNCOMPLETED

DAILY CALLS

1	X	—
2	X	—
3	X	—
4	X	—
5	X	—
6	X	—
7	X	—
8	X	—
9	X	—
10	X	—
11	X	—
12	X	—
13	X	—
14	X	—
15	X	—

"OOPS I FORGOT" - CARRY OVER TOMORROW

TO DO LIST #'S -

DAILY CALL #'S -

DAILY TASKS

DATE:

1	X	—
2	X	—
3	X	—
4	X	—
5	X	—
6	X	—
7	X	—
8	X	—
9	X	—
10	X	—
11	X	—
12	X	—
13	X	—
14	X	—
15	X	—
16	X	—
17	X	—
18	X	—
19	X	—
20	X	—
21	X	—
22	X	—
23	X	—
24	X	—
25	X	—

KEY: ☒ COMPLETED
☐ UNCOMPLETED

DAILY CALLS

① X —	② X —	③ X —
④ X —	⑤ X —	⑥ X —
⑦ X —	⑧ X —	⑨ X —
⑩ X —	⑪ X —	⑫ X —
⑬ X —	⑭ X —	⑮ X —

"OOPS I FORGOT" – CARRY OVER TOMORROW

TO DO LIST #'S –

DAILY CALL #'S –

DAILY TASKS

DATE:

① X —
② X —
③ X —
④ X —
⑤ X —
⑥ X —
⑦ X —
⑧ X —
⑨ X —
⑩ X —
⑪ X —
⑫ X —
⑬ X —
⑭ X —
⑮ X —
⑯ X —
⑰ X —
⑱ X —
⑲ X —
⑳ X —
㉑ X —
㉒ X —
㉓ X —
㉔ X —
㉕ X —

KEY: ☒ COMPLETED ☐— UNCOMPLETED

DAILY CALLS

① X —	② X —	③ X —
④ X —	⑤ X —	⑥ X —
⑦ X —	⑧ X —	⑨ X —
⑩ X —	⑪ X —	⑫ X —
⑬ X —	⑭ X —	⑮ X —

"OOPS I FORGOT" - CARRY OVER TOMORROW

TO DO LIST #'S -

DAILY CALL #'S -

DAILY TASKS

DATE:

① X —
② X —
③ X —
④ X —
⑤ X —
⑥ X —
⑦ X —
⑧ X —
⑨ X —
⑩ X —
⑪ X —
⑫ X —
⑬ X —
⑭ X —
⑮ X —
⑯ X —
⑰ X —
⑱ X —
⑲ X —
⑳ X —
㉑ X —
㉒ X —
㉓ X —
㉔ X —
㉕ X —

KEY: ☒ COMPLETED
⊟ UNCOMPLETED

DAILY CALLS

① X ⊟	② X ⊟	③ X ⊟
④ X ⊟	⑤ X ⊟	⑥ X ⊟
⑦ X ⊟	⑧ X ⊟	⑨ X ⊟
⑩ X ⊟	⑪ X ⊟	⑫ X ⊟
⑬ X ⊟	⑭ X ⊟	⑮ X ⊟

"OOPS I FORGOT" - CARRY OVER TOMORROW

TO DO LIST #'S -

DAILY CALL #'S -

DAILY TASKS

DATE:

① X ⊟
② X ⊟
③ X ⊟
④ X ⊟
⑤ X ⊟
⑥ X ⊟
⑦ X ⊟
⑧ X ⊟
⑨ X ⊟
⑩ X ⊟
⑪ X ⊟
⑫ X ⊟
⑬ X ⊟
⑭ X ⊟
⑮ X ⊟
⑯ X ⊟
⑰ X ⊟
⑱ X ⊟
⑲ X ⊟
⑳ X ⊟
㉑ X ⊟
㉒ X ⊟
㉓ X ⊟
㉔ X ⊟
㉕ X ⊟

KEY: ☒ COMPLETED
⊟ UNCOMPLETED

DAILY CALLS

1 ☒ ⊟	2 ☒ ⊟	3 ☒ ⊟
4 ☒ ⊟	5 ☒ ⊟	6 ☒ ⊟
7 ☒ ⊟	8 ☒ ⊟	9 ☒ ⊟
10 ☒ ⊟	11 ☒ ⊟	12 ☒ ⊟
13 ☒ ⊟	14 ☒ ⊟	15 ☒ ⊟

"OOPS I FORGOT" - CARRY OVER TOMORROW

TO DO LIST #'S -

DAILY CALL #'S -

DAILY TASKS

DATE:

1. ☒ ⊟
2. ☒ ⊟
3. ☒ ⊟
4. ☒ ⊟
5. ☒ ⊟
6. ☒ ⊟
7. ☒ ⊟
8. ☒ ⊟
9. ☒ ⊟
10. ☒ ⊟
11. ☒ ⊟
12. ☒ ⊟
13. ☒ ⊟
14. ☒ ⊟
15. ☒ ⊟
16. ☒ ⊟
17. ☒ ⊟
18. ☒ ⊟
19. ☒ ⊟
20. ☒ ⊟
21. ☒ ⊟
22. ☒ ⊟
23. ☒ ⊟
24. ☒ ⊟
25. ☒ ⊟

KEY: ☒ COMPLETED
☐ UNCOMPLETED

DAILY CALLS

① ☒ ☐
② ☒ ☐
③ ☒ ☐
④ ☒ ☐
⑤ ☒ ☐
⑥ ☒ ☐
⑦ ☒ ☐
⑧ ☒ ☐
⑨ ☒ ☐
⑩ ☒ ☐
⑪ ☒ ☐
⑫ ☒ ☐
⑬ ☒ ☐
⑭ ☒ ☐
⑮ ☒ ☐

"OOPS I FORGOT" - CARRY OVER TOMORROW

TO DO LIST #'S -

DAILY CALL #'S -

DAILY TASKS

DATE:

① ☒ ☐
② ☒ ☐
③ ☒ ☐
④ ☒ ☐
⑤ ☒ ☐
⑥ ☒ ☐
⑦ ☒ ☐
⑧ ☒ ☐
⑨ ☒ ☐
⑩ ☒ ☐
⑪ ☒ ☐
⑫ ☒ ☐
⑬ ☒ ☐
⑭ ☒ ☐
⑮ ☒ ☐
⑯ ☒ ☐
⑰ ☒ ☐
⑱ ☒ ☐
⑲ ☒ ☐
⑳ ☒ ☐
㉑ ☒ ☐
㉒ ☒ ☐
㉓ ☒ ☐
㉔ ☒ ☐
㉕ ☒ ☐

KEY: ☒ COMPLETED ⊟ UNCOMPLETED

DAILY CALLS

① X —	② X —	③ X —
④ X —	⑤ X —	⑥ X —
⑦ X —	⑧ X —	⑨ X —
⑩ X —	⑪ X —	⑫ X —
⑬ X —	⑭ X —	⑮ X —

"OOPS I FORGOT" - CARRY OVER TOMORROW

TO DO LIST #'S -

DAILY CALL #'S -

DAILY TASKS

DATE:

① X —
② X —
③ X —
④ X —
⑤ X —
⑥ X —
⑦ X —
⑧ X —
⑨ X —
⑩ X —
⑪ X —
⑫ X —
⑬ X —
⑭ X —
⑮ X —
⑯ X —
⑰ X —
⑱ X —
⑲ X —
⑳ X —
㉑ X —
㉒ X —
㉓ X —
㉔ X —
㉕ X —

KEY: X COMPLETED
— UNCOMPLETED

DAILY CALLS

① X —	② X —	③ X —
④ X —	⑤ X —	⑥ X —
⑦ X —	⑧ X —	⑨ X —
⑩ X —	⑪ X —	⑫ X —
⑬ X —	⑭ X —	⑮ X —

"OOPS I FORGOT" - CARRY OVER TOMORROW

TO DO LIST #'S -

DAILY CALL #'S -

DAILY TASKS

DATE:

① X —
② X —
③ X —
④ X —
⑤ X —
⑥ X —
⑦ X —
⑧ X —
⑨ X —
⑩ X —
⑪ X —
⑫ X —
⑬ X —
⑭ X —
⑮ X —
⑯ X —
⑰ X —
⑱ X —
⑲ X —
⑳ X —
㉑ X —
㉒ X —
㉓ X —
㉔ X —
㉕ X —

KEY: ☒ COMPLETED
⊟ UNCOMPLETED

DAILY CALLS

① X ⊟	② X ⊟	③ X ⊟
④ X ⊟	⑤ X ⊟	⑥ X ⊟
⑦ X ⊟	⑧ X ⊟	⑨ X ⊟
⑩ X ⊟	⑪ X ⊟	⑫ X ⊟
⑬ X ⊟	⑭ X ⊟	⑮ X ⊟

"OOPS I FORGOT" - CARRY OVER TOMORROW

TO DO LIST #'S -

DAILY CALL #'S -

DAILY TASKS

DATE:

① X ⊟
② X ⊟
③ X ⊟
④ X ⊟
⑤ X ⊟
⑥ X ⊟
⑦ X ⊟
⑧ X ⊟
⑨ X ⊟
⑩ X ⊟
⑪ X ⊟
⑫ X ⊟
⑬ X ⊟
⑭ X ⊟
⑮ X ⊟
⑯ X ⊟
⑰ X ⊟
⑱ X ⊟
⑲ X ⊟
⑳ X ⊟
㉑ X ⊟
㉒ X ⊟
㉓ X ⊟
㉔ X ⊟
㉕ X ⊟

KEY: ☒ COMPLETED
⊟ UNCOMPLETED

DAILY CALLS

① X — ② X — ③ X —

④ X — ⑤ X — ⑥ X —

⑦ X — ⑧ X — ⑨ X —

⑩ X — ⑪ X — ⑫ X —

⑬ X — ⑭ X — ⑮ X —

"OOPS I FORGOT" - CARRY OVER TOMORROW

TO DO LIST #'S -

DAILY CALL #'S -

DAILY TASKS

DATE:

① X —
② X —
③ X —
④ X —
⑤ X —
⑥ X —
⑦ X —
⑧ X —
⑨ X —
⑩ X —
⑪ X —
⑫ X —
⑬ X —
⑭ X —
⑮ X —
⑯ X —
⑰ X —
⑱ X —
⑲ X —
⑳ X —
㉑ X —
㉒ X —
㉓ X —
㉔ X —
㉕ X —

KEY: ☒ COMPLETED
☐— UNCOMPLETED

DAILY CALLS

① X —
② X —
③ X —
④ X —
⑤ X —
⑥ X —
⑦ X —
⑧ X —
⑨ X —
⑩ X —
⑪ X —
⑫ X —
⑬ X —
⑭ X —
⑮ X —

"OOPS I FORGOT" - CARRY OVER TOMORROW

TO DO LIST #'S -

DAILY CALL #'S -

DAILY TASKS

DATE:

① X —
② X —
③ X —
④ X —
⑤ X —
⑥ X —
⑦ X —
⑧ X —
⑨ X —
⑩ X —
⑪ X —
⑫ X —
⑬ X —
⑭ X —
⑮ X —
⑯ X —
⑰ X —
⑱ X —
⑲ X —
⑳ X —
㉑ X —
㉒ X —
㉓ X —
㉔ X —
㉕ X —

KEY: ☒ COMPLETED
     ⊟ UNCOMPLETED

DAILY CALLS

① X —	② X —	③ X —
④ X —	⑤ X —	⑥ X —
⑦ X —	⑧ X —	⑨ X —
⑩ X —	⑪ X —	⑫ X —
⑬ X —	⑭ X —	⑮ X —

"OOPS I FORGOT" - CARRY OVER TOMORROW

TO DO LIST #'S -

DAILY CALL #'S -

DAILY TASKS

DATE:

① X —
② X —
③ X —
④ X —
⑤ X —
⑥ X —
⑦ X —
⑧ X —
⑨ X —
⑩ X —
⑪ X —
⑫ X —
⑬ X —
⑭ X —
⑮ X —
⑯ X —
⑰ X —
⑱ X —
⑲ X —
⑳ X —
㉑ X —
㉒ X —
㉓ X —
㉔ X —
㉕ X —

KEY: ☒ COMPLETED
☐ UNCOMPLETED

DAILY CALLS

① X —	② X —	③ X —
④ X —	⑤ X —	⑥ X —
⑦ X —	⑧ X —	⑨ X —
⑩ X —	⑪ X —	⑫ X —
⑬ X —	⑭ X —	⑮ X —

"OOPS I FORGOT" - CARRY OVER TOMORROW

TO DO LIST #'S -

DAILY CALL #'S -

DAILY TASKS

DATE:

① X —
② X —
③ X —
④ X —
⑤ X —
⑥ X —
⑦ X —
⑧ X —
⑨ X —
⑩ X —
⑪ X —
⑫ X —
⑬ X —
⑭ X —
⑮ X —
⑯ X —
⑰ X —
⑱ X —
⑲ X —
⑳ X —
㉑ X —
㉒ X —
㉓ X —
㉔ X —
㉕ X —

KEY: ☒ COMPLETED
      ⊟ UNCOMPLETED

DAILY CALLS

① X ⊟	② X ⊟	③ X ⊟
④ X ⊟	⑤ X ⊟	⑥ X ⊟
⑦ X ⊟	⑧ X ⊟	⑨ X ⊟
⑩ X ⊟	⑪ X ⊟	⑫ X ⊟
⑬ X ⊟	⑭ X ⊟	⑮ X ⊟

"OOPS I FORGOT" - CARRY OVER TOMORROW

TO DO LIST #'S -

DAILY CALL #'S -

DAILY TASKS

DATE:

① X ⊟
② X ⊟
③ X ⊟
④ X ⊟
⑤ X ⊟
⑥ X ⊟
⑦ X ⊟
⑧ X ⊟
⑨ X ⊟
⑩ X ⊟
⑪ X ⊟
⑫ X ⊟
⑬ X ⊟
⑭ X ⊟
⑮ X ⊟
⑯ X ⊟
⑰ X ⊟
⑱ X ⊟
⑲ X ⊟
⑳ X ⊟
㉑ X ⊟
㉒ X ⊟
㉓ X ⊟
㉔ X ⊟
㉕ X ⊟

KEY: ☒ COMPLETED
☐ UNCOMPLETED

DAILY CALLS

① X ─
② X ─
③ X ─
④ X ─
⑤ X ─
⑥ X ─
⑦ X ─
⑧ X ─
⑨ X ─
⑩ X ─
⑪ X ─
⑫ X ─
⑬ X ─
⑭ X ─
⑮ X ─

"OOPS I FORGOT" - CARRY OVER TOMORROW

TO DO LIST #'S -

DAILY CALL #'S -

DAILY TASKS

DATE:

① X ─
② X ─
③ X ─
④ X ─
⑤ X ─
⑥ X ─
⑦ X ─
⑧ X ─
⑨ X ─
⑩ X ─
⑪ X ─
⑫ X ─
⑬ X ─
⑭ X ─
⑮ X ─
⑯ X ─
⑰ X ─
⑱ X ─
⑲ X ─
⑳ X ─
㉑ X ─
㉒ X ─
㉓ X ─
㉔ X ─
㉕ X ─

KEY: ☒ COMPLETED
⊟ UNCOMPLETED

DAILY CALLS

① X ⊟	② X ⊟	③ X ⊟
④ X ⊟	⑤ X ⊟	⑥ X ⊟
⑦ X ⊟	⑧ X ⊟	⑨ X ⊟
⑩ X ⊟	⑪ X ⊟	⑫ X ⊟
⑬ X ⊟	⑭ X ⊟	⑮ X ⊟

"OOPS I FORGOT" - CARRY OVER TOMORROW

TO DO LIST #'S -

DAILY CALL #'S -

DAILY TASKS

DATE:

① X ⊟
② X ⊟
③ X ⊟
④ X ⊟
⑤ X ⊟
⑥ X ⊟
⑦ X ⊟
⑧ X ⊟
⑨ X ⊟
⑩ X ⊟
⑪ X ⊟
⑫ X ⊟
⑬ X ⊟
⑭ X ⊟
⑮ X ⊟
⑯ X ⊟
⑰ X ⊟
⑱ X ⊟
⑲ X ⊟
⑳ X ⊟
㉑ X ⊟
㉒ X ⊟
㉓ X ⊟
㉔ X ⊟
㉕ X ⊟

KEY: ☒ COMPLETED
⊟ UNCOMPLETED

DAILY CALLS

① X —   ② X —   ③ X —

④ X —   ⑤ X —   ⑥ X —

⑦ X —   ⑧ X —   ⑨ X —

⑩ X —   ⑪ X —   ⑫ X —

⑬ X —   ⑭ X —   ⑮ X —

"OOPS I FORGOT" - CARRY OVER TOMORROW

TO DO LIST #'S -

DAILY CALL #'S -

DAILY TASKS

DATE:

① X —
② X —
③ X —
④ X —
⑤ X —
⑥ X —
⑦ X —
⑧ X —
⑨ X —
⑩ X —
⑪ X —
⑫ X —
⑬ X —
⑭ X —
⑮ X —
⑯ X —
⑰ X —
⑱ X —
⑲ X —
⑳ X —
㉑ X —
㉒ X —
㉓ X —
㉔ X —
㉕ X —

KEY: ☒ COMPLETED
☐ UNCOMPLETED

DAILY CALLS

① ☒ ☐ ② ☒ ☐ ③ ☒ ☐

④ ☒ ☐ ⑤ ☒ ☐ ⑥ ☒ ☐

⑦ ☒ ☐ ⑧ ☒ ☐ ⑨ ☒ ☐

⑩ ☒ ☐ ⑪ ☒ ☐ ⑫ ☒ ☐

⑬ ☒ ☐ ⑭ ☒ ☐ ⑮ ☒ ☐

"OOPS I FORGOT" - CARRY OVER TOMORROW

TO DO LIST #'S -

DAILY CALL #'S -

DAILY TASKS

DATE:

① ☒ ☐
② ☒ ☐
③ ☒ ☐
④ ☒ ☐
⑤ ☒ ☐
⑥ ☒ ☐
⑦ ☒ ☐
⑧ ☒ ☐
⑨ ☒ ☐
⑩ ☒ ☐
⑪ ☒ ☐
⑫ ☒ ☐
⑬ ☒ ☐
⑭ ☒ ☐
⑮ ☒ ☐
⑯ ☒ ☐
⑰ ☒ ☐
⑱ ☒ ☐
⑲ ☒ ☐
⑳ ☒ ☐
㉑ ☒ ☐
㉒ ☒ ☐
㉓ ☒ ☐
㉔ ☒ ☐
㉕ ☒ ☐

KEY: ☒ COMPLETED
⊟ UNCOMPLETED

DAILY CALLS

① X ⊟	② X ⊟	③ X ⊟
④ X ⊟	⑤ X ⊟	⑥ X ⊟
⑦ X ⊟	⑧ X ⊟	⑨ X ⊟
⑩ X ⊟	⑪ X ⊟	⑫ X ⊟
⑬ X ⊟	⑭ X ⊟	⑮ X ⊟

"OOPS I FORGOT" - CARRY OVER TOMORROW

TO DO LIST #'S -

DAILY CALL #'S -

DAILY TASKS

DATE:

① X ⊟
② X ⊟
③ X ⊟
④ X ⊟
⑤ X ⊟
⑥ X ⊟
⑦ X ⊟
⑧ X ⊟
⑨ X ⊟
⑩ X ⊟
⑪ X ⊟
⑫ X ⊟
⑬ X ⊟
⑭ X ⊟
⑮ X ⊟
⑯ X ⊟
⑰ X ⊟
⑱ X ⊟
⑲ X ⊟
⑳ X ⊟
㉑ X ⊟
㉒ X ⊟
㉓ X ⊟
㉔ X ⊟
㉕ X ⊟

KEY: ☒ COMPLETED
☐— UNCOMPLETED

DAILY TASKS

DATE:

① X —
② X —
③ X —
④ X —
⑤ X —
⑥ X —
⑦ X —
⑧ X —
⑨ X —
⑩ X —
⑪ X —
⑫ X —
⑬ X —
⑭ X —
⑮ X —
⑯ X —
⑰ X —
⑱ X —
⑲ X —
⑳ X —
㉑ X —
㉒ X —
㉓ X —
㉔ X —
㉕ X —

DAILY CALLS

① X —
② X —
③ X —
④ X —
⑤ X —
⑥ X —
⑦ X —
⑧ X —
⑨ X —
⑩ X —
⑪ X —
⑫ X —
⑬ X —
⑭ X —
⑮ X —

"OOPS I FORGOT" - CARRY OVER TOMORROW

TO DO LIST #'S -

DAILY CALL #'S -

KEY: ☒ COMPLETED
⊟ UNCOMPLETED

DAILY CALLS

1 ☒ ⊟	2 ☒ ⊟	3 ☒ ⊟
4 ☒ ⊟	5 ☒ ⊟	6 ☒ ⊟
7 ☒ ⊟	8 ☒ ⊟	9 ☒ ⊟
10 ☒ ⊟	11 ☒ ⊟	12 ☒ ⊟
13 ☒ ⊟	14 ☒ ⊟	15 ☒ ⊟

"OOPS I FORGOT" - CARRY OVER TOMORROW

TO DO LIST #'S -

DAILY CALL #'S -

DAILY TASKS

DATE:

1. ☒ ⊟
2. ☒ ⊟
3. ☒ ⊟
4. ☒ ⊟
5. ☒ ⊟
6. ☒ ⊟
7. ☒ ⊟
8. ☒ ⊟
9. ☒ ⊟
10. ☒ ⊟
11. ☒ ⊟
12. ☒ ⊟
13. ☒ ⊟
14. ☒ ⊟
15. ☒ ⊟
16. ☒ ⊟
17. ☒ ⊟
18. ☒ ⊟
19. ☒ ⊟
20. ☒ ⊟
21. ☒ ⊟
22. ☒ ⊟
23. ☒ ⊟
24. ☒ ⊟
25. ☒ ⊟

KEY: ☒ COMPLETED
☐— UNCOMPLETED

DAILY CALLS

① X —	② X —	③ X —
④ X —	⑤ X —	⑥ X —
⑦ X —	⑧ X —	⑨ X —
⑩ X —	⑪ X —	⑫ X —
⑬ X —	⑭ X —	⑮ X —

"OOPS I FORGOT" - CARRY OVER TOMORROW

TO DO LIST #'S -

DAILY CALL #'S -

DAILY TASKS

DATE:

① X —
② X —
③ X —
④ X —
⑤ X —
⑥ X —
⑦ X —
⑧ X —
⑨ X —
⑩ X —
⑪ X —
⑫ X —
⑬ X —
⑭ X —
⑮ X —
⑯ X —
⑰ X —
⑱ X —
⑲ X —
⑳ X —
㉑ X —
㉒ X —
㉓ X —
㉔ X —
㉕ X —

www.ingramcontent.com/pod-product-compliance
Lightning Source LLC
Chambersburg PA
CBHW081237180526
45171CB00005B/453